To Ma...

Be a conqueror

Elmer Towns

PRAYING WITH
THE CONQUERORS

PRAYING JOSHUA,
JUDGES, AND RUTH

BOOKS BY ELMER L. TOWNS

AVAILABLE FROM DESTINY IMAGE PUBLISHERS

PRAYING WITH THE CONQUERORS

PRAYING JOSHUA, JUDGES, AND RUTH

Praying the Scriptures Series

Elmer L. Towns

DEDICATION

To my editorial team who delivers my manuscripts to the publisher. Much of the series *Praying the Scriptures* was handwritten and they typed it into final form, proofread, and checked references—all to make it perfect. Sometimes I dictate stories, and even a few times I type on my computer laptop, but I couldn't do what I do, without them. Thanks to Linda Elliott for 13 years of working with my manuscripts. Also thanks to Trish Hicks, Kristin Wolfe, Dan Marchant, and Brittany Jenkins. Also thanks to my final reader—my wife, Ruth Towns. No matter how well I write, she always has good additions. Then finally, thanks to the great team at Destiny Image. You guys have done a fantastic job on these manuscripts.

CONTENTS

PREFACE

As you read this book, will you do what the title suggests? Will you *Pray With the Conquerors*? Most of the time we just read the Scriptures, which means we filter the message through our minds. But in this book you'll do more than that; as you pray through Joshua, Judges, and Ruth, you can join them in their victorious battles. You can triumph with them. My prayer is that this book will make you victorious in your Christian life. *Lord, may the readers enter a new experience of victorious living as they pray with Joshua, Judges, and Ruth.*

As Joshua fought military battles, you have spiritual battles to fight. You war against the world, the flesh, and the devil. You struggle against the lust of the flesh, the lust of the eyes, and the pride of life. The principles of Joshua's military campaigns can be followed by you. So pray with the conquerors to get spiritual victory.

You'll lose some battles, just as Jonathan lost the battle of Ai. You'll weep just as Joshua wept when he saw how sin in the camp led to the death of Israel's soldiers and Israel's defeat. So don't give up if you lose a battle against sin. To lose a battle is not losing the war. You must fight against a different place with different resources; but you can win. "He who is in you is greater than he who is in the world" (1 John 4:4).

Then too, there were a lot of defeats in the Book of Judges that led to bondage and slavery. That should motivate you to positive action. If you do not defeat sin, you will become its slave. Didn't Jesus tell us, "Whoever commits sin is a slave of sin" (John 8:34)? Remember, Jesus' promise of victory? "If the Son (Jesus Himself) makes you free, you shall be free indeed" (John 8:36). *Lord, I yield my whole life to You. I will not serve sin. I pray for victory.*

Pray the principles of warfare into your life. Learn them from these conquerors. Make them foremost in your life.

Slavery and death is the aim of our enemy, so fight with
all your might.

The battle is never won with half-hearted effort.

The battle is spiritual, so depend on God to fight in you
and through you.

Use all your weapons to their fullest potential—prayer,
Scripture, truth, righteousness, holiness, and the
spoken testimony of a forgiven believer.

Don't hide your testimony; let the Ark of the Covenant
go before you.

Have faith in God to do the miraculous.

Remember the overriding lesson from the Book of Judges: when you win a victory, don't quit doing the things that gained victory, or you'll be defeated in the next battle. Joshua conquered the land, but in Judges Israel stopped doing the spiritual things that gave them victory. "The people served the Lord all the days of Joshua, and all the days of the elders who outlived Joshua, who had seen all the great works of the Lord…then the children of Israel did evil in the sight of the Lord, and served Baals" (Judg. 2:7, 11). *Lord, keep me from sin, also keep my children and grandchildren true to You.*

As you read Judges, note that God raised them up to defeat a specific nation that had put part of Israel into bondage. Whereas Joshua conquered all the land of Israel from all her enemies; each judge only defeated one enemy and represented one tribe, or a combination of a few tribes. There's a lesson in this truth. Sometimes we are Joshua and we defeat all our enemies when we go to a church altar and dedicate ourselves to God for a complete victory. At other times we are a judge; we struggle with one specific temptation in only one area of our lives. *Lord, I pray with Joshua for a complete victory over all oppression, yet I realize sometimes the enemy slips into my life unnoticed and I must pray with a judge to defeat sin in one area of my life.*

As you pray through Judges, notice there is one weakness in each judge. (If Joshua had a weakness, we don't know what it is.) Othniel could be accused of nepotism, Ehud had a physical deformity, Deborah was a woman in a male-dominated society, Gideon was from the bottom of the social ladder, Jephthah was a half-breed son of a prostitute, and Samson, a womanizer. In spite of each weakness, God gave victory to each of them. That means God can use you in your uniqueness and weakness. As a matter of fact, the Lord loves to use weaknesses. "God deliberately chooses weak things...so that no one can ever boast in the presence of God" (1 Cor. 1:27,29 ELT). *Lord, in spite of my weakness, I trust in You to give me victory. Use me even though I am weak, for I depend on You.*

The Hebrew name Joshua is transliterated into the Greek *Yeshua*, which in English is Jesus. So when you pray with Joshua of the Old Testament, remember that Joshua is a picture of the victory that Jesus gives to us. You can also pray with Jesus Christ.

You can pray with Jesus because He dwells within your heart "that Christ may dwell in your hearts through faith" (Eph. 3:17). So praying in the faith of Jesus in you (see Gal. 2:20) becomes the basis of your faith— intercession before the Father. Then yield to Him, let His power flow through you for victory.

Also remember, you are in Christ. He stands at the right hand of the throne of the Father in Heaven. Jesus is making intercession for you (see Heb. 7:24-27). So pray with Jesus, and let your Savior present your prayers to the Father. Since Jesus is perfect and He knows the Father intimately, He can perfectly present your prayers so they will be heard and answered. *Lord, I come to You through Jesus. I pray for victory over the enemy without and I pray for victory over sin within. Give me strength to be a conqueror for You.*

May you pray better than ever before, because you are praying with the conquerors.

Sincerely yours in Christ,
Elmer L. Towns
Written from my home at the foot of the Blue Ridge Mountains
Winter 2008

PRAYING JOSHUA
FOR SUCCESSFUL SPIRITUAL WARFARE

INTRODUCTION

Joshua, the military leader, trimmed his beard with a sharp knife. He was different from Moses in every way. Whereas Moses had a long wiry grey beard—symbolic of Moses' wisdom and authority—Joshua's beard was cut short and stubbly. In battle, an enemy could grab a long beard for an advantage.

Moses knew the intricacies of the law; Joshua, a man of action, defended the law and applied the law. *Lord, I want to know both Your law and also apply it to my life.*

Moses was a spiritual leader who sacrificed a lamb and carried its blood into the Ark of the Covenant and the presence of God. Joshua, the fighter, needed a priest to sacrifice for him.

Today was the worst and best day in Joshua's life. Yesterday Moses died. His friend and companion for over 40 years had died. But today is the greatest day of Joshua's life, it's the day for which he was born, and the day for which God called and prepared him. Today, Joshua becomes the leader of 3 million Israelites. Today, Joshua prepares them to enter the Promised Land. Today, Israel is about to fulfill the promise God made to Abraham 600 years earlier. *Lord, may I be spiritually ready for the greatest day of my life.*

Today is the hinge of history. Six hundred years ago God's people were a nomadic tribe, living in tents, wandering in a strange land not knowing where they were going, looking for a city whose builder and maker is God (see Heb. 11:8-10). *Lord, I'm also looking for that city, even Heaven itself.*

Then Israel went to Egypt under the protection of Joseph, the Jewish Minister of Agriculture. During the next 300 years Israel became slaves in Egypt, suffering under oppressive persecution.

Then Moses led them victoriously out of Egypt to Mt. Sinai where the nation was organized to worship God.

Then Israel rebelled against God at Kadesh-Barnea and refused to enter the Promised Land. God promised that any male over 20 years of age would die. But today is absolutely new. Every Jew who came out of Egypt is dead, except Joshua and Caleb. All the slaves are buried in the desert because they rebelled against God, their unknown graves covered by the blowing sand. Yes, the old must die, and the new must spiritually conquer themselves, then they must conquer their enemies. *Lord, I must conquer my old nature so I can conquer the world, the flesh, and the devil.*

How Joshua begins his new day will determine his success in the coming days. Joshua will make the priority of Moses, his priority. First in Moses' life was talking to God and worshiping Him. Joshua went to his tent and folded the flap for privacy. He bowed before God, "The Lord spoke unto Joshua, the son of Nun, Moses' minister, saying 'Moses my servant is dead'" (Josh. 1:1-2).

Joshua thought, *There's the secret of Moses' success; God called Moses, "My servant." I too will be God's servant so I also will have success.*

Today is the most wonderful day of Joshua's life because God is talking to him as God talked to Moses. Now Joshua knows for sure that God wants him to lead Israel. God's word confirms it. *Lord, I too know You want to lead my life because Your Word—the Scriptures—confirms it to me.*

As each battle was fought, Joshua directed his dedicated soldiers (who had learned orderly and obedient marching in the wilderness). Joshua was a skilled strategist who understood that a small group of highly disciplined soldiers could defeat a larger army of lustful warriors who didn't understand the strength of discipline and order. *Lord, may I learn discipline and order in my private life.*

Joshua directed his army out of a divine consciousness that he was fulfilling the promises God made to Abraham (see Gen. 12:6-9). He had an awareness of divine sovereignty—since God had promised victory, he could not be defeated as long as he and his army were obedient to God. *Lord, I have that divine consciousness in my personal life.*

On three occasions, God supernaturally intervened to give His people victory. First, when Israel crossed the Jordan on dry land. This miracle happened when God used natural forces to produce a supernatural result—a landslide into the river upstream blocked the river flow. The miracle was God's timing, it happened when the priest stepped into the river. *Lord, I want Your timing in my life.*

The enemy who saw this miracle spread the word. Hence, every heathen soldier who picked up a sword against Israel knew in his heart they were fighting against the God who ruled nature. What an advantage for Israel. *Lord, fight for me as You fought for Israel.*

The second miracle was the collapse of the walls of Jericho. The Levites and soldiers marched around Jericho with the Ark of the Covenant. Did the walls fall down because of the vibration of soldiers marching, or because of the power of a sonic boom when they all shouted, or did God use a miracle? Maybe it was a divinely timed earthquake? Joshua doesn't tell us the answer in the text. Maybe because he didn't know. He only wrote what Israel experienced. *Lord, thank You for all the miracles You do in my life—miracles that I don't realize.*

The third miracle was the sun standing still in Heaven to give Joshua time to finish defeating the enemy. But what is a miracle? It's the divine intervention of the laws of nature for divine purpose. God wanted this evil nation eliminated, so He prevented them from running and hiding in the night, waiting for the sunlight of another day to fight again.

Some will question why Joshua and his army not only defeated his enemy, but he slaughtered them, wiping them out, down to the last child and old person. Some say a God of love wouldn't do this. They question the morality of the Israelite's fighting ways.

But look at the big picture. The Canaanites were so evil that they might have all committed the unpardonable sin. Noah had predicted and cursed the evil desire of Canaan, the head of the Canaanite race (see Gen. 9:24-27), and God had predicted the complete degeneracy of the Canaanite tribes (see Gen. 15:16). Archeology has demonstrated the carnage and sadism of the Canaanite people, and their unbridled sexual lust. Their god was Anak, the prostitute whose lust motivated their religion. Sexual deviancy was rampant and there was no fear of God in their eyes. God didn't want this evil practice to infiltrate His people. *Lord, protect me from evil when I can't protect myself.*

The apostle Paul wrote the Book of Romans to describe the sins of the heathen, which is a picture of the Canaanites, "Who, knowing the righteous judgment of God, that those who practice such things are deserving of death, not only do the same but also approve of those who practice them" (Rom. 1:32).

Every battle was not won with a miracle. Joshua does not saturate his book with indiscriminate miracles (like heathen mythologies). No, Joshua writes accurately as an eyewitness of those things that happened (see Josh. 24:26). If God performed other observable miracles, he would have included them. Since they are not included in his book, they probably didn't happen. But the phrase occurs repeatedly, "the Lord gave them victory" or "the Lord wiped them out." This meant God worked sovereignly through and with, and in each soldier; helping him fight, protecting him when he didn't know God was protecting him.

God also worked against the heathen soldiers, confusing their strategy, diminishing their strength, and blocking their progress in many small ways that human eyes couldn't see on the battlefield. Yet in hindsight, those who have experienced "God working all things together for good" (Rom. 8:28) realize inwardly how God helped Israel win each battle. *Lord, work through me as I fight against evil and satan's work.*

God Appoints Joshua as the New Leader

SCRIPTURE: JOSHUA 1

After Moses died, the Lord said to Joshua, "My servant Moses is dead. Now, you and all these people must cross over this Jordan River. Go into the land that I am giving to the people of Israel. I promised Moses that I would give you every spot where you walk in the land. All the territory—from the desert in the south to Lebanon in the north—will belong to you. All the land from the Great Euphrates River in the east, all the way to the Mediterranean Sea in the west will be your country. Joshua, as long as you live, no one will be able to defeat you. Just as I was with Moses, so I will be with you. I will always be with you; I will never abandon you. Be determined and brave. You will be the leader of these people so that they can conquer the land. This is the same land which I vowed I would give to their ancestors. Joshua, be strong and very brave. Be sure to obey all the teachings which My servant Moses commanded you. If you follow them exactly, do not turn neither to the right nor left; you will be successful in everything you do. You must always speak what is written in the Law of Moses, think about it day and night; make sure that you obey everything that is written there. If you do this, then you will prosper and be successful in every way. Be strong and brave. Do *not* be afraid or discouraged, because I—the Lord your God—am with you wherever you go."

So Joshua gave orders to the officers of the people, "Pass through the camp and tell the people: 'Prepare your food rations, because three days from now, you will cross over the Jordan River and you will be going in to conquer the land that the Lord your God is giving you to possess.'"

Then Joshua spoke to the people of Reuben, Gad, and the half-tribe of Manasseh, saying, "Do you remember what Moses the servant of the Lord charged you? He said: 'The Lord your God will give you rest; He will give you the land east of the Jordan River. Your wives, little children, and animals can settle here. However, all your fighting men must prepare for war and cross over the Jordan River ahead of your Hebrew brothers. You must help them conquer the land. The Lord has already given you a place to rest. He will do the same thing for your Hebrew brothers. But you must help them until they conquer the land to the west of here. That is the land that the Lord your God is giving them. Then you will be permitted to return to your own land that is east of the Jordan River. This is the land that Moses, the servant of the Lord gave to your people." Then the people answered Joshua, saying, "Everything that you command us to do, we will do. Wherever you send us, we will go. Just as we obeyed Moses, we will obey you. We know that the Lord your God is with you just as He was with Moses. Anyone who resists your commands or disobeys anything that you command will be put to death. Just be strong and be brave."

Moses' Death

The Lord spoke to Joshua…saying: "Moses My servant is dead. Now therefore, arise, go over this Jordan, you and all this people, to the land which I am giving to them" (Joshua 1:1-2).

God told Joshua, "Moses is dead." Joshua and the people didn't know this because Moses died on the top of Mount Nebo. How could they know for sure except God told them? Then the people mourned personally for Moses, but they probably also experienced some panic, because they were leaderless. "Who will protect us?" they asked. Maybe Israel felt "our enemies will devour us without Moses' miracles." While they grieved, Moses was enjoying the presence of God, just as when you grieve over the loss of a loved one, they're with the Lord. *Lord, help me understand Your perspective of death.*

So why do people fear death? Because death is a shadow and what's hidden in the shadows scares us. We usually die in pain; and none of us are good with pain. So we fear pain, and death scares us. So when you step into that scary shadow of death, remember what David said, "Yea, though I walk through the valley of the shadow of death, I will fear no evil; for You are with me" (Ps. 23:4). There's that thought again, *with me*. In death you'll encounter the Lord because He'll be with you. *Lord, help me remember Your presence.*

How do you tell someone a loved one has died? Joshua knew Moses went up into Mount Nebo, but he and the people didn't know what happened to their leader. Since God had buried Moses up on Mount Nebo, God had to be the One to tell them, "Moses is dead." God told Joshua in a straightforward way, "Moses my servant is dead." God, who is able to keep us from death, allowed Moses to die; just as He'll allow you to die. Why? Because God has appointed a time when all of us will die. Be comforted because your death will not catch God by surprise. *Lord, I know You have a time when I'll come to be with You.*

God didn't just say, "Moses is dead." He added a possessive phrase, "Moses my servant." It's almost as if God had tears in His eyes when Moses died. Was God sorry that Moses died? No, because it was better for Moses to be with God. While on earth, Moses was God's servant. Moses walked by faith, he'd do anything God commanded. Moses served God every way he could. As a result, God constantly called Moses *His servant*. It would be almost 400 years until God had another servant who was as gifted and devoted as Moses. Four hundred years after the death of Moses, God would have another servant, David, a man after God's own heart.

How do you tell someone that a loved one has died? There's no way to sugarcoat the news. I was told, "Your son has been in a terrible accident, and he was killed instantly." I had to know about his death, and there was no easy way to tell me or anyone else about the death of a loved one. Once you tell them, back off. Let them internalize the news. The loss of anyone precious leaves a gaping hole in their life. They need time to grieve and heal. "The children of Israel wept for Moses...thirty days" (Deut. 34:8).

After the death of a loved one—any death—life goes on, so must you. You can't grieve forever. God told Joshua "Arise." You have to leave the cemetery; you must turn your face toward the future and its problems. Moses was gone, but the immediate problem for Israel was the river Jordan. And it wasn't just a river; it was springtime, the river was flooding out of its banks. Israel faced an insurmountable barrier. "Got any rivers you think are uncrossable?" Just as God manifests His presence in death, He also manifests Himself in solving problems, and overcoming barriers. What problems do you face? Have you looked for God's presence? He's available! *Lord, I've got a river.*

Israel had been waiting for 40 years to enter the Promised Land. Couldn't they wait several more weeks until the spring flood went down? No! God commanded, "Go over this Jordan." The phrase *this Jordan* suggests Joshua was looking at his obstacle when God commanded him to cross it. Not wait! Not go around it! Cross it now!

If they waited, or they went around the barrier, Israel would have solved their problem in the flesh. But God wanted to manifest Himself to His people. God wanted Israel to rely on Him, not on Moses, not Joshua. It was as if God was saying, "You have Me—not Moses—let's go!" *Lead on, Lord.*

When God told Joshua that Moses was dead, He also told Joshua to take *this people over Jordan.* This part of the conversation suggests Joshua was standing in front of the multitude when he got the message about Moses. The former leader was gone, and now the multitude needed a new leader. "As I was with Moses, so I will be with you" (Josh. 1:5). There you have the phrase again, *with you.* After the death of a loved one, you have to go on, and God will be with you. His presence is the one force that will help you get through your grief and help you go on with your life. As God was with your loved ones, He'll be *with you. Lord, I need You today.*

Joshua's Strength

This Book of the Law shall not depart from your mouth, but you shall meditate in it day and night, that you may observe to do according to all that is written in it. For then you will make your way prosperous, and then you will have good success (Joshua 1:8).

Joshua had two gigantic needs in his life. He was grieving because Moses, his lifelong friend and coworker has just died. His first need was comfort. Also, God told Joshua to lead the people over the uncrossable Jordan and conquer the infidels who inhabit the Promised Land. Joshua's second need was supernatural leadership ability. To overcome his grieving, Joshua needed the *presence* of God in his heart, and to conquer the land Joshua needed the *power* of God in battle. How does God meet his needs? God points Joshua to the Scriptures, "Meditate in it day and night." God promised that when Joshua internalized the Scriptures, "the Lord your God is with you wherever you go" (Josh. 1:9). *Lord, I need to see You in the Scriptures.*

Maybe you can't feel God's presence today. If not today, surely there have been days or seasons when God's presence seemed far away. When you can't feel God in prayer, remember He is as close as your Bible—you'll meet God in His Word. Why? "All Scripture is given by inspiration of God" (2 Tim. 3:16). The word *inspiration* means "God-breathed." God breathes His Spirit into the words of Scripture. Too often we think inspiration only means the accuracy of the Bible. It does mean that every word is put there by God, but inspiration also means the words of the Bible are filled with God's life-giving presence because His Spirit lives in His Word. *Lord, I find You in the Scriptures.*

When you put the words of Scripture in your heart, you place God at the center of your life. You can do it by memorizing the Bible. No matter what age, you can memorize God's Word. Joshua was told to do it, and he was past 80. How old are you? *Lord, I'll never be too old for Your Word.*

First you memorize God's Word, then you meditate on what you've learned. When God's Word fills your thoughts, He is in your mind to guide your thinking. Remember, successful thoughts lead to successful living. Also, when God controls your thoughts, you become godly. And when God's love controls your outlook, you become more loving.

Joshua learned that when God is at the center of one's thinking, he could be courageous (see Josh. 1:6), successful (see Josh. 1:8), and victorious (see Josh. 1:9). One person plus God is a majority. What problems do you face today, and how is your outlook on life? Do you have a defeated attitude? A pessimistic attitude? God can make you a winner, so what do you have to do? Get God's Word in your mind and let it guide your thoughts. *Lord, I will fill my life with Your Word.*

We all make many decisions each day, some as insignificant as what shoes to wear. Other decisions are life directing. Wouldn't you like God's help to make them? God may not audibly whisper into your ear the answer to every decision; but if His Word has saturated your mind, then He will automatically be present to guide the decisions you make. Think about it, God will be present to mold and direct every decision—not just the big ones—if you memorize and meditate on His Word. And that's better than waiting for a whisper in the dark night when you're scared to death. *Lord, I will do what You say in Scripture.*

To get God's presence with you today, remember these two commands, "memorize and meditate." God promised Joshua, "As I was with Moses, so I will be with you" (Josh. 1:5). God promises to be with you, just as he was with Moses, if you memorize and meditate. *Lord, I will do it.*

You can't have one without the other. Some little children memorize verses in Sunday school—a lot of verses—but they became prodigals from God when they grew up. Why? Because they had the Bible in their mind, but not in their lives. Without meditation, you don't let God influence and control your life.

There's an opposite extreme. Some try to meditate about God, but they do it without the Scriptures. They try to think about God, and some thoughts come, but the right thoughts don't always come. Because "out of the heart proceed evil thoughts, murders, adulteries, fornications, thefts, false witness, blasphemies" (Matt. 15:19). *Lord, I will memorize the Scriptures to counteract the evil of my heart.*

When your heart is controlled by God-thoughts, you are not likely to miss God or deny God. You need the Scriptures to keep you on track. So to have a balanced thought life, remember that memory and meditation go together. *Lord, I will do both.*

Your *life steps* come from your thoughts. What you plan to do in your mind, is usually reflected in the path you take in life. "A man's heart plans his way" (Prov. 16:9) and "As he thinks in his heart, so is he" (Prov. 23:7). So you need God's presence in your heart to point out the best path for today. He's there to speak to you when you read and meditate on His Word. He's there when you let the Scriptures guide your problem solving. He's as close to you as the Word of God to influence all you do. *Lord, I'm reaching now for my Bible.*

Rahab Helps the Two Spies

SCRIPTURE: JOSHUA 2

Joshua, the son of Nun, sent out two spies from Shittim secretly. He
said to them, "Go, look over the land closely, especially the city
of Jericho." So the men went to Jericho and to the house of a
prostitute and stayed there. This woman's name was Rahab.
Someone told the king of Jericho: "Listen, some men from the
Israelites have come here tonight. They are spying on the land."
So the king of Jericho sent this message to Rahab: "Bring out the
men who came and entered your house, because they have come
to spy on our land!"

However, the woman had hidden the two men. She said, "Yes, they did
come here, but I didn't know where they came from. It was getting dark when they closed the city gate and the men left. I don't
know where they went. Run quickly after them, maybe you can
catch them." But the woman had taken the men up to the roof
and hidden them under stalks of flax. She had spread the flax
out on the roof to dry. So, the king's men chased after them.
They went to the places where people cross the Jordan River.

Before the Hebrew spies lay down to sleep that night, Rahab went up
to them on the roof and said, "I know that the Lord has given
this land to your people. You terrify us. Everyone who lies in this
land is melting with fear as we wait for you to invade us. We
have heard how the Lord dried up the waters of the Red Sea
when you came out of Egypt. We have also heard what you did
to King Sihon and King Og, how you completely destroyed
those two Amorite kings who lived east of the Jordan River. And
when we heard this, we became very scared. Now our men are

afraid to fight you. This is because the Lord your God is the true God in the heavens above and on the earth below. So now, I beg you, make a vow to me by the Lord to promise that you will show kindness to my family just as I showed you kindness. Give me a token that you will keep the truth of your word. Promise me that you will allow my whole family to stay alive. Save the lives of my father, my mother, my brothers, my sisters, and all of their families from death."

The men agreed. They said, "Do not tell anyone what we are doing. When the Lord gives us the land, we will be loyal to you. You can trust us."

Rahab's home was built into the city wall. She lived within the wall. So, she used a rope to lower the men down through a window. She said to them, "Go into the hills. Those who are chasing you will not find you there. You must hide there for three days. After the searchers return, you can go on your way."

The Jewish men said to her, "You must do as we tell you. If you don't, we cannot be responsible for keeping our vow. You are using a red rope to help us escape. When we return to this land, you must tie this red rope in this particular window. Assemble your father, mother, brothers, and entire family into your house. We can keep everyone safe who stays inside this house. If anyone in your house is hurt, we will be responsible. If anyone goes outside your house into the street and is killed, it is his own fault. We cannot be responsible for him. But you must not tell anyone about this pact. If you do, we are free from it" (literally, "We will be guiltless from our oath which you made us promise").

Rahab answered, "I agree to this." So she sent them away, and they left. Then she tied the red rope in that window. The Jewish men left and went into the hills, staying there for three days. The king's men searched for them all along the road, but they never found them. So they went back to Jericho. Then the two men began their return trip, coming down from the hills and crossing over the Jordan River. Then they went to Joshua, the son of Nun, to report to him everything that had happened to them. They said to Joshua, "The Lord has certainly put all of the land into our grasp. All the people who live in that land are melting with fear before we even invade them."

The Miraculous Crossing

SCRIPTURE: JOSHUA 3

Early the next morning, Joshua and all the Israelites left Shittim and traveled to the Jordan River and camped there for the night. After three full days, the officers passed through the camp giving these orders to the people: "You will see the Levitical priests carrying the Ark of the Covenant of the Lord your God. Then you must leave where you are and begin following it. That is how you will know which direction to go. You have never traveled this way before. However, you must not follow the Ark of the Covenant too closely. You must stay about one half mile behind the Ark of the Covenant." Then Joshua told the people, "Make yourselves holy for God, because tomorrow the Lord will do amazing things among you."

And Joshua said to the priests: "Pick up the Ark of the Covenant and prepare to cross over the river ahead of the people." So, the priests picked up the Ark of the Covenant and went ahead of the people. Then the Lord said to Joshua, "Today I will begin to make you a great man. It will be obvious to all the Israelites. The people will know that I am with you, just as I was with Moses. The priests are now carrying the Ark of the Covenant. Give them this command: 'Go to the edge of the water of the Jordan River and stand there.'" Then Joshua said to the Israelites, "Come here, listen to the words of the Lord your God. Here is proof that the living God is with you. Here is proof that He will force out the Canaanites, the Hittites, the Hivites, the Perizzites, the Girgashites, the Amorites, and the Jebusites. Listen—the Ark of the Covenant will go ahead of you into the

Jordan River. It is your covenant with the Lord of the whole world.

"Now select 12 men for yourselves. Choose one man from each of the 12 tribes of Israel. The priests are carrying the Ark of the Lord, the Lord of the whole world. They will carry it into the Jordan River ahead of you. When the bottoms of their feet touch the waters of the Jordan, the river will stop flowing. The water will be stopped (literally, the waters coming from upstream will stand up in one huge mass.)" So, the people left the place where they had camped. The priests were carrying the Ark of the Covenant ahead of them, as they prepared to cross the Jordan River.

Now, during harvest time (April or May), the Jordan River is in flood stage, overflowing its banks. So the river was very wide (perhaps 150 yards across from the rains of spring and the melting snows of Mount Hermon, which happens annually.) The priests who were carrying the Ark came to the Jordan River and stepped into the water. Just at that moment, the water stopped flowing. It stood up in a mass a great distance away—far north of the town of Adam (20 miles upstream). The water that normally flows to the Sea of Arabah, the Dead Sea, was completely cut off. Then the people crossed over the river opposite Jericho.

The priests carried the Lord's Ark of the Covenant to the middle of the river and stopped there. The ground was dry. They waited there until all the nation of Israel had walked across the Jordan River on dry land.

The Lesson of the River Bottom

And as those who bore the ark came to the Jordan, and the feet of the priests who bore the ark dipped in the edge of the water (for the

*Jordan overflows all its banks during the whole time of harvest),
that the waters which came down from upstream stood still...Then
the priests who bore the ark of the covenant of the Lord stood firm
on dry ground in the midst of the Jordan; and all Israel crossed over
on dry ground* (Joshua 3:15-17).

A re you facing something that's too big for you? Something impossible? What has God asked you to do that's overwhelming? God told
Joshua and Israel to cross the Jordan but the river was flooding. They
could have gone around the Dead Sea to enter the land, or they could
have waited until the flood was over. But either option was disobedience,
because God said, "Go over this Jordan" (Josh. 1:2.) *Lord, help me not run
away from my challenges.*

When Israel obeyed and the priest stepped into the water, at that
moment God sent an earthquake upstream to dam up the waters. Where
the flooded Jordan flowed, a landslide blocked the river. Circumstantial?
No! Providential? Yes! God's hand that controls the power of earthquakes, responded to the faith of 3 million people. The priests carrying
the Ark were spiritual representatives of all Israel when they stepped into
the water. God's timing was miraculous. *Lord, I want Your power and
timing in my life.*

There's a deeper lesson here than the miracle. Have you seen it? The Ark
is more than the symbolic mercy seat of redemption. God dwells between
the cherubim; He sits on the mercy seat (see Exod. 25:22.) When the Ark
was taken into the river, the priests were taking God into the water. God
was in the river bottom. What is the lesson? When you are overwhelmed
with a problem, step into the water with God's presence. See what God
can do. *Lord, I'm ready to step.*

Can you see faith in this picture? When the priest shouldered the Ark, the
threatening floodwater was rushing by. When the priest began walking
toward the river all Israel was watching. Did they doubt? How could
they? God was being transported toward the watery obstacle. In faith the
priest waded into the water. In faith Israel trusted God to do something.
After all, their fathers told them about the Red Sea parting and about

water coming out of the rock and other miracles. Now was their time to experience the miraculous. *Lord, today it's my turn.*

Did you notice what comes first? Did the water stop flowing before they stepped into the riverbed? No! Did they step into the water before the miracle occurred? Yes! What does that tell you? Don't wait for God to solve your problem before you begin to act. If you are facing a gigantic hindrance, pray and commit your problem to God. Invite His presence into the problem. Then commit yourself to the action that God would have you take. Commit yourself to glorifying God. Then act, knowing the presence of Christ in your heart will see you through. *Lord, I'm stepping.*

The priests had *participatory faith*. The Ark was on their shoulders, and they bore the load. They walked into the water. The people standing ready had *observatory faith*. They watched the Ark being carried into the water. They saw the waters recede, and they benefited from the miracle. They walked across the Jordan, carrying all their belongings and their families. For three million people to enter the Promised Land, both *participatory faith* and *observatory faith* were necessary. In your walk of faith, there will be times when you personally will bear the burden of God's command and God's presence. You must act. You must participate with God in faith. At other times, you will get the benefit of someone else's faith. You believe God will do it, but you're not the leader. You have *observatory faith*. *Lord, I need both kinds of faith.*

Notice where God was located in this scene. God was sitting on the Ark as it sat on the shoulders of the priests. In one sense, God is everywhere present at the same time. So, God could have gone before Israel into the waters to make them a way. But that's not how it was done. God was on the shoulders of the priests and they carried Him into the flood. You don't have to worry about God drowning, nor do you have to worry about the priests drowning. They're with God. A partnership of God and the priests can't be defeated. *Lord, teach me to walk with You.*

What about yourself? Paul tells us, "We then, as workers together with Him" (2 Cor. 6:1.) Isn't *together* a wonderful word? Even when we are afraid—together with God—we will win. In our flesh, we may lose, but God never loses; He always wins.

36

One more lesson, "the whole nation crossed." When you take God into your problem, other people are blessed. The priest shouldered the Ark, but they did more than get themselves and God across the river. The whole nation crossed. Will other people be blessed because of your obedience? *Lord, may I bless others today.*

The first persons to go in the river were the last to come out. The priests were leaders. In an act of faith, they waded into the waters first. Then as leaders, the priests remained in the dry river bottom until everyone else crossed to safety. They stayed in danger's path, but they were not threatened because God was with them. Then when everyone had crossed, they came out of the riverbed, and the waters returned. If you're going to lead for God, you have to take the first step of faith and you have to remain faithful until the last. You must face more danger, take more risks, and have more courage. But it's worth it because you'll have God's presence with you in the river bottom. *Lord, here I come into the waters.*

The Twelve Stones

SCRIPTURE: JOSHUA 4

The whole nation (3 million people) finished crossing the Jordan River.
Then the Lord spoke to Joshua: "Pick 12 men, one man from
each tribe. Command the men to pick up 12 large stones from
the middle of the Jordan River, taking them from the very spot
where the priests had stood. Carry the stones with you and put
them down where you spend the night tonight." So Joshua
confirmed one man from each tribe. Then he summoned the
12 men from the people of Israel, saying to them, "Go out into
the middle of the Jordan River where the Ark of the Lord your
God was positioned. Each of you must find one large stone.
Carry that stone on your shoulder, one stone for each tribe of
Israel. These stones will be a sign among you. In the future, your
children will ask you: 'What do these stones mean to you?' Tell
them: 'The Lord stopped the water from flowing in the Jordan
River ahead of the Ark of the Covenant of the Lord. As the Ark
entered the Jordan River, the water stopped flowing.' These
stones will help the Israelites remember this forever."

So the 12 men of Israel obeyed Joshua. They carried 12 stones from the
middle of the Jordan River, one stone for each of the 12 tribes
of Israel, just as the Lord had told Joshua. They carried the
stones with them and put them down where they set up their
camp.

Next Joshua also erected a pile of 12 stones in the middle of the Jordan
River. He put them where the priests had stood while carrying
the Ark of the Covenant. These stones are still there today.

(Perhaps 20 years after this event, the Book of Joshua was written.)

The Lord had commanded Joshua to tell the people what to do. (It was what Moses had directed Joshua to do.) So, the priests who were carrying the Ark continued to stand in the middle of the Jordan River until everything was finished. The people continued hurrying across. When all the people had finished crossing over, the priests carried the Ark of the Lord to the other side, as the people watched. The men from the tribe of Reuben, from the tribe of Gad, and from the eastern half-tribe of Manasseh crossed the river ahead of the Israelites. They were obeying what Moses had told them. They were prepared for war. An army of about 40,000 soldiers was ready to fight. They passed by the presence of the Lord (where the Ark of the Covenant of the Lord was located), as they marched across the river. Then they went toward the plains of Jericho to go to war.

That day, the Lord made Joshua a great man in the sight of all Israel. They respected Joshua for the rest of his life, just as they had respected Moses.

Then the Lord spoke to Joshua: "Command the priests to bring up the Ark of the Covenant out of the Jordan River." Then Joshua commanded the priests: "Come up out of the riverbed!" So the priests brought the Ark of the Covenant of the Lord out of the middle of the Jordan River. As soon as their feet touched the bank, the water began flowing again. The Jordan River overflowed its banks once more. It was exactly as it had been before they crossed.

The people came up out of the Jordan River on the 10th day of the 1st month. (This was the same day in the Jewish calendar, during the month of Nisan, when the Passover lamb was to be selected. See Exodus 12:3.) They camped at Gilgal, on the eastern boundary of Jericho. They carried with them the 12 stones that had been taken out of the Jordan River. And at Gilgal (about two miles northeast of ancient Jericho), Joshua set up those stones as a monument. Then he spoke to the Israelites saying, "In the future, your children will ask you: 'What do these stones mean?' This is what you will tell them: 'Israel crossed the Jordan River on dry ground here. The Lord your God caused the water to stop flowing. The river was dry until the people finished crossing it. The Lord your God did the same thing for us at the Jordan River that He had done for the people at the Red Sea. He stopped the water at the Red Sea ahead of us until we had crossed over. The Lord did this so that all the people of the land would know His strength; it is very powerful. You must always revere the Lord your God.'"

Circumcising the Jewish Men

SCRIPTURE: JOSHUA 5

So, the Lord dried up the waters of the Jordan River in front of the
Israelites until they had crossed it. And, all the kings of the
Amorites west of the Jordan River heard about that. All the
Canaanite kings living beside the Mediterranean Sea heard about
it, too. They were very afraid and had no courage left to fight the
invading Israelites.

At that time, the Lord spoke to Joshua, "Make flint-knives. Restore the
circumcision for this new generation of Jewish males (thus
reestablishing continuity of the covenant relationship with God
through Abraham) of the Israelites." So, Joshua made flint-
knives. The men were circumcised at Gibeath-Haarloth.

This is why Joshua circumcised the males: After the Hebrew people
came out of Egypt, all the men who were old enough to serve in
the army died in the desert. The men who had come out of
Egypt had been circumcised, but all those who were born in the
desert had not been circumcised.

The Israelites had moved around in the desert for 40 years. During that
time all the fighting men who had left Egypt had died. This was
because they had not obeyed the Lord. So the Lord vowed that
they would not see the land, even though this was the land He
had promised to give their ancestors. It was a land flowing with
milk and honey. That is why their sons replaced them, but none
of the boys who were born during the trip from Egypt had been
circumcised. So Joshua had them circumcised. After all had

finished being circumcised, they stayed in the camp in their places until they healed.

Then the Lord spoke to Joshua: "As slaves in Egypt, everyone looked down on you, but today I have removed that stigma." So Joshua named that place "Gilgal." (The Hebrew verb for "roll," *galal*.) And, it is still called "Gilgal" even today.

Celebrating the Passover Meal

The people of Israel were camping at Gilgal, on the plains of Jericho on the evening of the 14th day of the month, when they celebrated the Passover Feast. (The nation of Israel had not done this for about 40 years [Num. 9:1-5].) The next day after the Passover, the people ate some of the food that grew in that land; bread made without yeast and roasted grain. When they ate this native grain, the manna stopped coming the very next day. The Israelites received no more manna from God. They ate the food that grew in the land of Canaan that year.

Joshua's Personal Encounter

Joshua was near Jericho when he looked up and saw a Man standing in front of him. The Man had a sword in His hand. Joshua went to him and asked, "Are you a friend or an enemy?"

The Man answered, "I am neither. I have come now as the Commander of the Lord's army." Then Joshua laid down on the ground face-down and worshiped Him. Joshua asked, "Do You have a command for me?"

The Commander of the Lord's army answered him, "Take off your sandals from your feet, because the place where you are standing is holy." And Joshua did so.

Joshua Meeting Jesus

And Joshua went to Him and said to Him, "Are You for us or for our adversaries?" So He said, "No, but as Commander of the army of the Lord I have now come." And Joshua fell on his face to the earth and worshiped, and said to Him, "What does my Lord say to His servant?" (Joshua 5:13-14).

Have you ever tried to convince God to bless something you were doing or about to do? Have you ever tried to get God on your side? When you were attempting something that was difficult or frightening, have you ever begged God to be with you? That's what Joshua was doing. Joshua was preparing to attack and defeat the evil city of Jericho—a seemingly impossible task. Then Joshua met the Lord, and he recognized it was the Lord. Joshua thought the man he encountered was a soldier, perhaps an enemy soldier, or perhaps one of his soldiers he didn't recognize. Perhaps Joshua thought the man was some kind of heavenly soldier, like a fighting angel. Joshua wanted to enlist the soldier to fight for him. But it was the Lord whom Joshua met. It was the Lord who wanted to enlist Joshua in His battle. You don't get God on your side, the reverse must happen. You must get on God's side. *Lord, where do I sign up?*

Joshua came up against a huge barrier; he was facing his enemy, "Joshua was by Jericho" (Josh. 5:13.) As a soldier, Joshua was probably spying out the city to find its weaknesses, or a niche where he could attack. Joshua's strategy was not wrong because we make good decisions based on good information, and we need data to lay out life's strategy. But when the obstacle was present, so was the Lord. Remember when you face a barrier, God is nearby. Maybe you can't see Him, just as Joshua didn't know who the warrior was. But the Lord was there. *Lord, thank You for being near even when I don't recognize You.*

Joshua didn't recognize the soldier, so he asked, "Are you for us, or our enemy?" If Joshua hadn't drawn his sword, his hand was probably near the handle. It's an admirable trait to be ready—always—to fight. Are you ready for an attack from the enemy today? *Lord, I'm ready.*

The soldier was, "The Commander of the Army of the Lord." This was a Christophany—an appearance of Christ in the Old Testament. Since we cannot see the Father or the Holy Spirit, this appearance of deity was obviously Jesus in a pre-incarnate appearance. When Joshua realized he was standing in the presence of deity, he did what any of us would do. Joshua stopped asking questions, and fell to his face. Are you ready to stop questioning God and fall to your face? *I yield to You.*

Jesus comes to us to solve our problems in our time of need. He came to Joshua as a soldier, because Joshua was facing a battle. To some Jesus comes as a Physician to heal, as a Teacher to instruct, as a Shepherd to lead, or He comes as a Counselor to help solve problems. But Joshua saw a man with sword drawn ready for battle. What Joshua needed was help in fighting the biggest battle of his life. He wanted this soldier on his side because Joshua was planning an attack and a fierce battle. Have you got an attack plan for today, and you've come to get God's help? There may be an easier way than fighting. *Lord, help me today.*

Jesus had an easier way to capture Jericho. Israel was to carry the Ark of God's presence once around the city for seven days. Then on the last day they were to go around the city seven times, then blow trumpets. When they obeyed, God would send a miracle to destroy the walls so they could capture the city. God's way was a lot easier and would save more lives. So Joshua had a choice, do it his way or God's way. You face the same question. Are you going to solve today's problems your way or God's way? Do you still want God to bless your plans, or are you willing to fit into God's plans? *Lord, show me Your plans for this day.*

The answer is obvious. You want to get on God's side. So how does that happen? What must you do? Do what Joshua did, "He fell at his feet and worshiped." When you fall at Jesus' feet, you allow Him to be your Lord. When you worship, you magnify Him. *Lord, I do it now.*

Before you fight, you must worship. That means you put God at the right place in your life. Before you rush into today's battle, make sure to retreat into His presence. Like Joshua, you may find an easier way to win your battle in God's presence. Joshua began looking at his enemy in Jericho, but ended up looking at his Lord. For in the presence of the Lord, you get your battle strategy, your battle courage (assurance), and your battle goal. *Lord, help me win.*

This was the first battle in the Promised Land. It had to be successful or the other battles would also fail. The spiritual approach to this battle would shed light on how the others could be won. Every lesson Joshua learned in this first battle would be a foundation on which to build. So this battle was the most important one of all. He needed to be on God's side and follow God's strategy. Joshua needed God to fight for him. So what did he do? He worshiped. And to win today's battle, what must you do? Worship! *Lord, I worship!*

The Fall of Jericho

SCRIPTURE: JOSHUA 6

The city of Jericho was closed, and the gates were barricaded. They were
expecting the Israelites to attack. No one went into the city. And,
no one came out.

Then the Lord spoke to Joshua, "I have given to you Jericho, its king,
and all of its fighting men. March around the city with all your
army once each day. Do this for six days. Have seven priests
carry seven trumpets made from the horns of male sheep. Tell
them to walk in front of the Ark. On the seventh day, you must
march around the city seven times, tell the priests to blow the
trumpets as they march. Then they must blow one long blast on
their trumpets. When you hear that sound, have all the people
shout extra loudly. Then the walls of the city will fall down. And
each soldier of the army will go straight ahead into the city."

So Joshua, the son of Nun, summoned the priests and told them, "Pick
up the Ark of the Covenant. Let seven priests carry the seven
trumpets and march in front of the Ark." Then Joshua commanded the people, "Now go, march around the city. The soldiers with weapons will march in front of the Ark of the Lord."

After Joshua spoke to the people, the seven priests began marching
ahead of the Lord's Ark. They moved on with the seven trumpets
and blew them as they marched. The priests carrying the Ark of
the Covenant of the Lord followed them. The soldiers with
weapons marched in front of the priests, and some armed men
walked behind the Ark too. The priests were blowing their trumpets continually. Now Joshua had commanded the people not to

give a war cry, saying, "Do not shout. Do not say a word until the moment I tell you. Then, shout!"

So the Ark of the Lord went around the city one time, and returned to the camp and spent the night there.

Early the next morning, Joshua got up, and the priests carried the Ark of the Lord again around the city. The seven priests carried the seven trumpets made of rams' horns in front of the Ark of the Lord, blowing their trumpets continually as they went. The soldiers with weapons marched in front of them, the other soldiers walked behind the Ark of the Lord. All this time, the priests were blowing their trumpets. So on the second day, they marched around the city once, and went back to the camp. They did this every day for six days.

On the seventh day, they arose at dawn. They marched around the city just as they had done on the six previous days. However, on that day they marched around the city seven times.

On the seventh time around, the priests blew their trumpets in one long blast. Then Joshua gave the command: "Now, shout! The Lord has given this city to you! The city and everything in it are to be dedicated as an offering to the Lord. Only Rahab the prostitute and everyone in her house should remain alive—they must not be killed. That is because Rahab hid the two spies whom we sent out. You must not take any of the things that are to be dedicated as an offering to the Lord. If you take such things, then you yourselves will be destroyed. You would also cause much trouble for the entire camp of Israel and put us under a curse. All the silver, and gold, and the things made from bronze and iron belong to the Lord. They are to be set aside for the Lord. They will go into His special treasury."

When the priests blew the trumpets with a long blast, and the people heard that, they shouted. When the trumpets blasted and the people shouted extra loud, the walls fell down. Each soldier of the army ran straight ahead into the city. The Israelites captured Jericho. They completely destroyed every living thing in the city, and killed every man and woman, even the young people and the old people. They killed all the cattle, the sheep, and the donkeys, too.

Joshua told the two men who had spied on the land: "Go into the prostitute's house and bring her out and all of her people who are with her. This is because of the oath that we swore to her." So the two young spies went into that house and brought Rahab out. They also brought out her father, mother, and brothers, and all those relatives who were with her. They put her entire family in a safe place, outside the camp of Israel.

Then the Israelites burned the whole city and everything in it. However, they did not burn the silver, or the gold, or the things made of bronze or iron. They put these things into the Tabernacle of the Lord. Joshua spared Rahab the prostitute, her family, and all those individuals who belonged to her. This was because Rahab had helped the messengers whom Joshua had sent to spy on Jericho. Rahab still lives among the Israelites today. (At the time that the Book of Joshua was written.)

Then Joshua made this solemn prediction: "Anyone who tries to rebuild this city of Jericho will be punished by a curse from the presence of the Lord. The man who lays the foundation of this city will lose his oldest son. The man who sets up the gates will lose his youngest son." (See the fulfillment of this in First Kings 16:34, and Hiel in the time of King Ahab, about 550 years later.) So the Lord was with Joshua, and he became famous throughout all the land.

Jericho's Defeat

And the armed men went before them. But the rear guard came after the ark of the Lord, while the priests continued blowing the trumpets (Joshua 6:13).

What is the biggest problem you face today? Do you face a small conflict, or something life-threatening? Don't face it alone; make sure you have the presence of God with you. Joshua had to conquer a formidable stronghold. Jericho was one of the most fortified cities in the then known world. For if Joshua couldn't conquer Jericho, he couldn't capture the surrounding territory. *Lord, I have a problem.*

When Joshua met Jesus in a Christophany, he received the formula for victory—march in a parade around Jericho each day. Start the soldiers marching, then have some priests follow blowing trumpets. Next take God around the city—let the priests bear the Ark of the Lord on their shoulders in a parade around Jericho. Show the enemy that God is on your side. Parade around the city once each day for six days, but march around it seven times on the seventh day. Then everyone shout and charge to conquer the city. *Lord, help me see Your plan to solve my problem.*

This simple story of military strategy has many lessons that will help you win today's victory. Notice how God told Joshua to take soldiers with the priests when they marched around the city. Be prepared. Look out for premature attacks from enemy soldiers who could come out of the city to attack the priests. Even when you are trusting God to help you, do all you can to protect yourself. Don't expose yourself needlessly to danger. *Lord, I will prepare.*

Joshua needed patience. Victory didn't come after initial obedience on the first day's march around Jericho. Each day for six days, Israel had to follow orders...correct formation...correct march...correct obedience. The victory didn't come gradually with continued obedience. No! Israel obeyed each day with no visual results. Sometimes you have to obey when you see nothing happening in the conflict you face. If you've got the Lord with you, and you're following His directions, keep marching. A seventh-day victory is coming. *Lord, I look forward to eventual victory.*

They blew the trumpets daily. That's like using our mouths to testify to other people. The priests were sounding the trumpets to get the attention of everyone in Jericho. Sometimes you want the world to know you're trusting God, sometimes you don't. Trying to scare the enemy was a usual military tactic in Old Testament times. Wasn't it foolhardy to blow a trumpet at Jericho, instead of waving swords and warning the enemy? Not when you've got the Ark with you, because you've got God on your side. You don't need tricks. The presence of God should be enough to warn them. But the enemy didn't surrender. They didn't believe God made a difference. Are you controlled by your unbelief? *Lord, You're with me, help me obey.*

The soldiers of Jericho heard the trumpets. What did the enemy see when they ran to the wall? They saw a box carried on the shoulders of priests. Israel was testifying that its strength was in the God of the Box. In case any people in Jericho missed the parable of the first day, they could see the spectacle the following day. Do you have faith to show them the Lord each day? *Lord, give me faith and patience.*

Why seven times on the seventh day? Because seven represented Israel's perfect obedience. Because seven kept the complete attention of Jericho. Because seven is God's favorite number. Because seven announced the end, just like the seventh day is the end of a week. If you're going through conflict, an end is coming. You don't know when…how…or where; but God knows and God will end it in His way. *Lord, I trust You.*

The Ark was carried around the city seven times. They obeyed the God who was traveling with them. He was not sitting on a hill safely off in the distance, watching and waiting to do something. God was in the march; He went seven times around the enemy. He knew experientially the terrain. He saw the walls up close. God is in your conflict with you. He doesn't just stay back at the place where you met Him in your morning watch. Your quiet time in God's presence means as much to God as to you. He leaves "your prayer closet" with you, and enters your conflict with you. You go with God, so what do you need? *Lord, I need confidence.*

The people and God worked together for victory. When the people shouted, God destroyed the walls. Would one shout alone bring down the walls? I think not. Would God have brought down the walls without the people's shout? He could have, but probably wouldn't have, because God works in response to our faith. "For assuredly, I say to you, whoever says to this mountain, 'Be removed and be cast into the sea'...he will have whatever he says" (Mark 11:23.) *Lord, I speak Your victory.*

There is strength in united faith. Notice all Israel was commanded to shout. I doubt if any kept silent. And how did they shout? The Living Bible describes it, "They shouted as loud as they could." Total enthusiasm, total obedience, total faith. Then every soldier charged straight ahead, total victory. *Lord, help me obey You in every way.*

Victory came when Israel did exactly what God commanded, God and man working together. That's how you'll win over your conflict. You must work together with God. You must do everything humanly possible to solve the problem, praying to God daily as you symbolically walk around the walls that block your progress. Take God with you as you approach your problem, just as Israel took the Ark with them. Then move ahead when the walls come down, taking charge. "We work together as partners who belong to God" (1 Cor. 3:9 TLB). *Lord, let's go.*

The Sin of Achan

SCRIPTURE: JOSHUA 7

However, the Israelites sinned a great sin regarding the forbidden
   things. There was a man named Achan, from the tribe of Judah,
   who was the son of Carmi and the grandson of Zimri and the
   descendant of Zerah. Achan stole some of the things that
   belonged to the Lord. The Lord became very angry at the
   Israelites. *Lord, I remember You said, "Thou shalt not steal."*

Joshua sent some men from Jericho to Ai. (An uphill trek of about
   15 miles. The total population of Ai was about 12,000 people
   [see Josh. 8:25].) Ai was near Beth-Aven, east of Bethel. He told
   them: "Go up to Ai and spy on that area." So the men went to
   spy on Ai.

Later, they came back to Joshua and said, "There are only a few men in
   Ai. We do not need all of our army to defeat them there. Merely
   send up 2,000 or 3,000 men to strike down Ai. There is no
   need to send all of our forces." So only about 3,000 men of the
   army went up to Ai. But the people of Ai defeated the Israelites
   badly. The men of Ai chased them from the city gate all the way
   to the Shebarim. (Meaning the rock bluffs that overlooked the
   Jordan Valley.) They killed about 36 Israelites, striking them
   down on the slopes, as they were going down the hill. The
   courage of the Israelite army failed. They became very afraid.
   Lord, remind me that private sin of one hurts all.

Then Joshua tore his clothes (a sign of deep emotional distress) to show
   how upset he was. And he lay on the ground facedown in the
   presence of the Ark of the Lord. He stayed there until evening,

with the elders of Israel. They also threw dirt upon their heads to show that they were very depressed. *Lord, may I retreat to You when facing defeat and destruction.*

Then Joshua said, "O Lord, the One Who is Always Present, You clearly brought our people across the Jordan River. Why did you bring us this far and then permit the Amorites to defeat us? I wish we would have been content to settle down on the other side of the Jordan River! O Lord, there is nothing I can say. Israel has been beaten by its enemies. The Canaanites and all the other people who live in this country will hear about this. They will surround us (Joshua feared that the combined forces of the Canaanite armies might trap the Israelites up against the west bank of the Jordan River) and kill us all. Then what will You do for Your own great Name?" *Lord, may I never blame You for my sin or the sin of others.*

The Lord interrupted Joshua, "Stand up! Why are you lying down on your face? Israel (the Jewish people were a "divinely constituted organic whole") has sinned. They have also broken My covenant which I commanded them to obey. They violated the ban. They have stolen from Me. They have lied, too. They have taken those forbidden things and put them among their own possessions. That is why the Israelites cannot defeat their enemies. Instead, they turned from the fight and ran away. They have come under condemnation. I will not be with you again, if you do not destroy these forbidden items from among you!" *Lord, don't take Your presence from me.*

"Now go. Have the people separate themselves from sin for Me. Tell them: 'Dedicate yourselves to the Lord in preparation for tomorrow. The Lord, the God of Israel, says: "Forbidden items are among you, O Israel. You will never defeat your enemies until you get rid of those things from among you."' Tomorrow morning, you must all stand accountable to the Lord. You must officially present yourselves to God. All the tribes must stand in My presence, one by one. The Lord will show (God may have revealed this by the Urim and Thummim from the ephod vest of the high priest [see Exod. 28:30; 1 Sam. 2:28; 14:41]) which tribe has sinned. Then that tribe must stand alone before God. Then the Lord will show which clan has sinned. Then that clan must stand alone before Him. Then the Lord will look at that family, person by person. The one who has stolen the forbidden items will be set on fire along with everything that belongs to him. He has broken the covenant of the Lord. He has done a shameful thing among the people of Israel." *Lord, I am terrified to stand in Your presence with sin in my life without the covering of the blood of Christ.*

Early the next morning, Joshua led all of Israel into the presence of the Lord. Each of the tribes stood in the presence of God, and He chose the tribe of Judah. So, all the clans of Judah stood before the Lord and He chose the clan of Zerah. Then all the families of Zerah stood before the Lord, and He chose the household of Zimri.

Then Joshua told all the men in that household to come before the Lord, one by one. And the Lord chose Achan, the son of Carmi. *Lord, sin cannot hide from You.*

Then Joshua said to Achan, "My son, you should tell the truth. Confess to the Lord, the God of Israel. Tell me what you have done. Do not try to hide anything from me." *Lord, I will always confess my sin.*

Then Achan answered, "It is true. I have sinned against the Lord, the God of Israel. This is what I did: among the plunder in Jericho, I saw a beautiful robe from Babylonia. And I saw 200 shekels of silver (about five pounds of silver) and a big bar of gold that weighs more than one and a quarter pounds. I wanted those things very much, so I took them. You can find them buried in the ground in the middle of my tent. The silver is on the bottom of it." *Lord, when I hide my sin, You withhold Your blessing and punish me for my sin.*

So Joshua sent some messengers who ran to the tent. They found it hidden there, the silver was underneath it. The men brought it all out of the tent and carried it to Joshua and all the Israelites. Then they laid those forbidden things out on the ground in the presence of the Lord.

Then Joshua and all the people led Achan, the descendant of Zerah, to the valley of Achor. They took the silver, the robe and the big bar of gold, and Achan's sons, daughters (because Achan's offspring knew about the theft, but did not report it), his bulls, his donkeys, his flock, his tent, and everything he owned. Then Joshua said, "You caused so much trouble for us, but today the Lord will bring trouble on you." Then all the people of Israel threw stones at Achan (stoned him with stones) until he died. They also killed his family members with stones. Then the people burned them. They piled rocks on top of Achan's corpse. (That large pile is still there today.) This is why it is called "The Valley of Achor" until this day. After this, the Lord was no longer angry. *Lord, thank You that Jesus died for my sin so I don't have to die.*

Achan's Sin

Achan...took of the accursed things; so the anger of the Lord burned against the children of Israel...Then Joshua...fell to the earth...before the ark of the Lord...and Joshua said, "Alas, Lord God, why have you brought this people...to deliver us into the hand of the Amorites, to destroy us..." (Joshua 7:1,6-7).

Have you ever blamed God for your troubles? Oh, you didn't outright say God did it, but you make it sound like He was responsible. Maybe God didn't answer a prayer, so you complained. Maybe things went bad so you asked God why He didn't interrupt events or change circumstances. Since God has all power, and He didn't solve your problem, it's easy to blame Him.

One man stole money and clothes from Jericho—God told Israel not to keep anything—so Israel lost its next battle. God didn't fight for Israel in the battle against Ai like he did in Jericho. Because Israel was defeated at Ai, Joshua blamed God. *Lord, forgive me when I've blamed You.*

Why is it we have such a hard time taking responsibility for our actions? Why do we want to blame someone else for our failure? The answer is simple. God made us responsible creatures. It's the essence of why He created us. God gave us the responsibility to worship Him, to obey Him, to trust Him. God made us responsible to Him; and when we fail, we must answer to Him.

But as human beings we don't like being accountable for our actions. We want to be exalted; we want to be "Number One." So when we fail, it's embarrassing. When we're no longer "Number One," what do we do? We blame someone else because it makes us "Number One" again. Blaming someone else can become a habit because we always want to be on top. Blaming others can be self-satisfying. *Lord, forgive me for blaming others for my mistakes.*

God was with Israel when the nation defeated Jericho. He led them into battle when the Ark was carried forward by the priests. So when Israel fought its second battle against a smaller city that had fewer soldiers, the nation of Israel naturally expected to win. Have you ever won a great spiritual battle, yet the next day fall flat on your face? Was it God's fault or yours? *It was my fault, Lord.*

Israel lost the battle against Ai, but notice what Joshua had not done. Before the first battle of Jericho, Joshua prayed, but the Bible says nothing about prayer before the second battle against Ai. Israel sent the priests—with the Ark of God—into the first battle. The Bible says nothing about the priests at Ai and nothing about the Ark. Does that mean the presence of God didn't go with them? Did Israel fail because she didn't trust God? *Lord, I've failed in the past because I forgot You.*

If Joshua had prayed and if Israel had God's presence with them at Ai, maybe God would have convicted them of the hidden sin of Achan before the battle. Maybe they wouldn't have been defeated. But they lost, and 36 good soldiers died needlessly. Why? Because of what the leaders didn't do and because of what one man did. He sinned. Have you ever been defeated because you didn't pray or seek God's presence? Have you ever lost a battle because of sin? Did you blame God? *Lord, I'm sorry.*

Experiencing the presence of God is the most important thing in your Christian life. And losing His presence is tragic. When the Bible describes "grieve the Holy Spirit" (Eph. 4:30), it means we allow the existence of conscious sin in our life. We sin and don't confess it and we don't repent. We sin and don't feel sorry. But the Spirit is grieved over just one sin, which means God sorrows. Next the Bible describes, "Do not quench the Spirit" (1 Thess. 5:19.) Quench means to *put out* or *extinguish.* When you quench your thirst, you *put it out.* When you quench the Spirit of God, you flaunt your sin and extinguish the flame of any Christian testimony you might have had. If you have an outward sin that's eroding your testimony, deal with it. If you have a secret sin, get rid of it before it grows into bigger problems. Like Israel, don't lose a battle because of a hidden sin. *Lord, I confess my sins...*

Achan tried to hide his stolen treasure in a hole under a rug in his tent, but God brought it to full view. If you try to hide your secret sin, God will bring it to full light. Notice the opposite. If you confess your sin publicly, God will forgive it, and bury it in the deepest sea (Mic. 7:19).

This lesson begins with blaming God for your sin (He's never the cause of your sin), but ends up blaming yourself. When it comes to sin, the bottom line is losing the presence of God. When you sin, don't confess just to feel good or to be successful. You confess to restore God's presence in your life. Then you will experience God's peace that comes with His presence. And after you confess your sin and come back to God, then worship Him. When you enter His presence, take off your shoes and worship Him, for you're on holy ground (see Josh. 5:15.) *Lord, I'm coming back to worship.*

Ai Is Captured and Destroyed

SCRIPTURE: JOSHUA 8

Then the Lord spoke to Joshua, "Do not be afraid. Do not give up. Go up to Ai. Arise and take all your fighting men with you. I will help you defeat the king of Ai. I am giving to you his people, his city, and his land. You must do to Ai and its king what you did to Jericho and its king. Only this time you may take all its plunder and its animals. You may keep it for yourselves. Set up an ambush behind the city."

So Joshua and his whole army arose and went to Ai. Then Joshua chose 30,000 of his best fighters, and he sent these men out at night. Joshua gave them these orders: "Listen carefully. You must set up an ambush behind the city. Do not go very far away from it. All of you must be alert. I and the men who are with me will advance on the city. The men in the city will come out to fight us as they did before. Then we will turn and run away from them. They will chase us away from the city as we run away from them. They will think that we are running away from them as we did before. At that time, you must come out from your ambush position and capture the city. The Lord your God will give you the power to win. After you capture the city, set it on fire. Make sure that you carry out the Lord's command! Look, I have given you your orders."

Joshua sent them away, and they went to hide at their ambush position. They stayed in a place between Bethel and Ai, to the west of Ai. But Joshua spent the night among his main army.

Early the next morning, Joshua gathered his men together, and with the
elders of Israel went up to Ai. The people of Ai could clearly see
them. All of the soldiers who were with Joshua marched up to
Ai. They got closer and closer. Then they stopped in front of the
city and camped just north of Ai. There was a valley between
them and the city. Then Joshua selected about 5,000 men. (It is
possible that these 5,000 men constituted a second ambush
unit, or perhaps were supposed to protect their flank against a
potential threat from Bethel.) He set them up as an ambush in
the area that was west of the city, between Bethel and Ai. So the
Jewish army took their positions. The main camp was north of
the city. The other men were hiding to the west. That night,
Joshua went down into the middle of the valley.

When the king of Ai saw the army of Israel, he and his men got up
early the next morning and hurried out to fight them.
(Apparently, the king of Ai was trying to surprise Joshua's men
by an early first strike.) He and all his army went out to a place
east of the city. But the king of Ai did not know that Jewish soldiers were waiting as an ambush against him behind the city.
Joshua and all the men of Israel allowed the army of Ai to push
them back. Then they ran east toward the desert. All the men of
the army in Ai were ordered to chase Joshua and his men. So
they left the city and went after Joshua and his army and chased
Israel. Therefore, the city was left open. Not even one man
stayed behind to protect it. Then the Lord said to Joshua, "Point
the spear that is in your hand toward Ai, because I will deliver it
into your hand." So Joshua pointed the spear that was in his
hand toward the city of Ai. The Israelites who were part of the
ambush saw Joshua stretch out his hand. So they suddenly came
out of their hiding place and rushed toward the city. They easily
entered the city and seized it. Then they quickly set the whole
city on fire.

When the men of Ai looked back, behold, they saw smoke rising into the sky from their city. At the same time, the main Jewish army stopped running and turned back against the men of Ai who had been chasing them. The men of Ai could not escape in any direction. Joshua and all his men realized that the ambush group had captured the city when they saw the smoke of the city going up. So they stopped running and turned around to counterattack the men of Ai. The Israelite men who ambushed Ai also came out of the city to fight the men of Ai from the rear. The men of Ai were caught between the two armies of Israel. The Israelites killed them all—not one of the men of Ai was left alive. None of the men of Ai escaped.

However, Joshua's men did catch the king of Ai alive, and they brought him to Joshua. During the fighting, the army of Israel chased the men of Ai into the fields and into the desert. The Israelites killed all of them. After they finished, they went back to Ai and also killed everyone there. That day, all the people of Ai died— 12,000 men and women.

Joshua held out his spear toward Ai. (This act was a signal to his smaller army to destroy the city. It is possible that some sort of flay may have been attached to his spear.) He did not pull back his spear until all the people of Ai were completely wiped out.

This time, the troops of Israel kept the animals for themselves. They also seized the plunder of that city. This is what the Lord told them to do when He gave the order to Joshua. Joshua burned up the city of Ai and it became a permanent pile of ruins. Joshua hanged the king of Ai on a tree. He left him hanging there until evening. As the sun was going down, Joshua told his men to take the king's dead body down from the tree. He told them to throw it down at the city gate which was now open. Then they piled a huge heap of large rocks on top of his corpse. It is still there today (at the time when the Book of Joshua was written.)

An Altar Is Built on Mount Ebal

Then Joshua built an altar to the Lord, the God of Israel, on Mount Ebal. Moses, the Lord's servant, had commanded the Israelites to do this. Joshua built the altar as it was described in the Book of the Law (Torah) by Moses. (See Deuteronomy 27:1-8.) The altar was made from whole field stones that were not cut. (No human tool was used on them.) The Israelites offered whole burnt offerings to the Lord on that altar. They also sacrificed peace offerings. There Joshua made a copy of the Law of Moses by inscribing it on stones. He did this for all the Israelites to see. All Israel—the elders, the officers, the judges—were present. They were standing around the Ark of the Covenant of the Lord. They stood facing the Levitical priests who had carried the Ark. Israelites and non-Israelites were all standing there. Half of the people stood in front of Mount Ebal. The other half stood in front of Mount Gerizim. This was the way the Lord's servant, Moses, had originally commanded the people to be blessed.

Then Joshua read all the words of the Law of Moses. He read the blessings and the curses. (See Deuteronomy 27-28.) He read it exactly as it was written in the Book of the Law (Torah.) Joshua read out loud every single instruction that Moses had given. This happened in front of all the Israelites who were gathered together. All the women and the little children where there, as well as all the non-Israelites who had associated themselves with God's people.

The Gibeonites Trick Joshua

Scripture: Joshua 9

All the kings west of the Jordan River heard about these things. They
were the kings of the Hittites, the Amorites, the Canaanites, the
Perizzites, the Hivites, and the Jebusites. They lived in the mountains, on the foothills, and all along the whole Mediterranean
seacoast, as far as Lebanon. All these kings joined forces to fight
against Joshua and the Israelites.

The people who lived in the town of Gibeon also heard about what
Joshua had done to Jericho and Ai. So they decided to trick the
Israelites. They got some old wine bags that were cracked and
patched up. And they put them in some old saddlebags on their
donkeys. Then they traveled as a delegation with worn-out,
patched-up sandals. And they wore raggedy old clothes. In addition, they took along some dry, moldy crumbs of bread. They
came to Joshua at the campsite near Gilgal and said to Joshua
and the men of Israel, "We have traveled from a land that is far
away. Make a peace treaty with us now."

The men of Israel said to these Hivites, "How could we make a pact
with you? (This was forbidden to the Jews [see Exod. 23:32;
34:12; Deut. 7:2].) Maybe you live near us?"

The Gibeonites said to Joshua "No, we are your servants."

But Joshua asked, "Who are you? And, where do you come from?" Then
the men answered him, "We, your servants have come from a
country that is very far away. We came because we heard of the
name of the Lord, your God. He's famous! (The Gibeonites

pretended to be moved by religious motives; namely, their desire to worship the true God.) We heard about everything He did in Egypt. We have also heard about all that He did to the two kings of the Amorites—Sihon (the king of Heshbon) and Og (the king of Bashan) who was king in Ashtaroth. They were on the east side of the Jordan River. So our elders and all the people who live in our land told us: 'Take food for your trip, and go to meet the Israelites. Say to them: "We are your servants. Make a peace treaty with us now. Look, this is our bread. On the day we left home to travel here, it was still warm and fresh. But now, it is dry and moldy. And here are our wine bags. When we left home, they were new when we filled them with wine. But now, look, they are old and cracked. And these are our old clothes and our old sandals. They are almost worn out from such a long journey."'"

The men of Israel tasted the old bread. However, they did not consult the Lord about it. So Joshua made peace with them, and he made a treaty of friendship with the people of Gibeon. He agreed to let them live. The leaders of the Hebrew community made a vow to honor the pact.

Three days later, after they had made the pact with them, the Israelites learned that the Gibeonites were their neighbors—they lived nearby. So the Israelites went over to where the Gibeonites lived (about 20 miles from Gilgal). On the third day, the Israelites arrived at their cities (Gibeon, Chephirah, Beeroth, and Kiriath-Jearim), but the Israelites did not attack those cities, because the leaders of the Jewish community had made a solemn promise to the Gibeonites by the Lord, the God of Israel. The whole Jewish community complained against the leaders who had made that pact. But the chiefs answered, "We have given our word by the Lord, the God of Israel. We cannot attack them now. This is what we'll do: We must let them live. We cannot kill them, or else God's punishment will be upon us, because we would be breaking the vow that we made to them." So the leaders said to the Jewish community, "Let the Gibeonites live, but they will cut wood and carry water for our entire community"—just as the leaders had agreed with the Gibeonites.

Then Joshua summoned the Gibeonites, saying, "Why did you lie to us? You claimed that your country was very far away, yet you live nearby. Now, you are condemned; you will become our slaves. You will always have to cut wood and carry water for the house of my God."

The Gibeonites answered Joshua, "We lied to you because we feared for our very lives. We received reliable information that the Lord your God had commanded His servant Moses to give all of this land to your people and to wipe out all the people in your path who live in this land. Now, listen, we are in your hands. You may do with us whatever you wish. You may do anything to us that you think is right."

So Joshua agreed; he spared their lives. He did not allow the Israelites to kill them. But on that day, Joshua did make the Gibeonites slaves to the Israelites. The Gibeonites cut the wood and carried the water for the Jewish community. And the Gibeonites would continue doing all those tasks for the altar of the Lord— wherever He chose that place to be. They are still doing this today. (That is, at the time the Book of Joshua was written, perhaps 20 years after this event.)

The Amorites Are Defeated

SCRIPTURE: JOSHUA 10

Adoni-Zedek, the king of Jerusalem, heard that Joshua had captured Ai
and completely destroyed it, along with its king. He heard that
Joshua had done the same thing to Jericho and its king. Adoni-
Zedek also learned that the Gibeonites had made peace with
Israel. The Gibeonites lived near Jerusalem (about six miles
away.) Adoni-Zedek and his people were very afraid. Why?
Because Gibeon was a big city, like one of the cities that had a
king. Gibeon was bigger than Ai, and all of its men were good
fighters. So Adoni-Zedek the king of Jerusalem, sent a message
to Hoham the king of Hebron, to Piram the king of Jarmuth, to
Japhia the king of Lachish, and to Debir the king of Eglon, saying: "Come up to me and help me. Let us attack the city of
Gibeon because Gibeon has made peace with Joshua and the
Israelites." Then those five Amorite kings joined forces. They
were: the king of Jerusalem; the king of Hebron; the king of
Jarmuth; the king of Lachish; and the king of Eglon. All their
armies came to the city of Gibeon. They surrounded it and
attacked it.

The Gibeonites sent an urgent message to Joshua at his camp at Gilgal,
saying, "We are your servants. Don't let us be destroyed. (The
peace treaty with the Gibeonites obligated the Israelites to come
to the aid of the Gibeonites.) Come up to us quickly and save
us. Help us. All the Amorite kings living in the hill-country have
joined their forces against us."

So Joshua marched up from Gilgal—he and his whole army, his best
fighting men were with him. The Lord spoke to Joshua, "Don't

be afraid of those Amorite armies. I will put them into your
hands. Not a single one of them will be able to stand up to
you."

Then Joshua and his army did a forced march all night to Gibeon from
Gilgal. (It was 26 miles from Gilgal to Gibeon, an uphill climb
of about 2,000 feet. Normally, that distance was covered by a
three-day journey [see Josh. 9:17].) The Lord confused the
Amorites ahead of the Israelites; and the Amorites panicked. The
Lord struck them down with a lot of bloodshed at Gibeon. The
Lord chased them on the road going up to Beth-Horon.
The Lord killed men all the way to Azekah and Makkedah.
As the Amorites ran away from the Israelites, coming down from
the hill at Beth-Horon on the way to Azekah, the Lord showered
huge hailstones upon the Amorites from the sky, killing them. In
fact, more men were killed by the hailstones than were killed
with the swords of Israel.

Joshua stood in front of the whole army of Israel and spoke to the
Lord.

"O sun, stand still over Gibeon. O moon, stop over the Valley of
Aijalon." So the sun stood still.

And the moon stopped, until the nation of Israel could take vengeance
upon their enemies.

That day, the Lord handed over the Amorites to the Israelites. (These
words are written in the Book of Jashar, an ancient collection of
songs mentioned in Second Samuel 1:18-27.)

The sun stopped in the middle of the sky. It did not hurry to go down
for an entire day. There has never been such a day—before or
after—like that day. The Lord listened to a human being, because
the Lord was fighting on behalf of Israel.

During the battle, these five kings ran away. They hid in a cave near
Makkedah (Joshua's temporary headquarters.) But someone
found the five kings, hiding in that cave, and told Joshua about
it. So Joshua ordered: "Close up the opening to the cave with big
rocks and put some men there to guard the kings. But, you soldiers don't stay there. Keep chasing after your enemies. Attack
them from the rear. Don't let them arrive at their cities safely.
Why? Because the Lord your God has delivered them into your
hands."

So Joshua and the Israelites finished slaughtering them; it was a huge
defeat. The Amorites were wiped out. Only a few survivors
reached their strong-walled cities. After the conflict, all the army
returned safely to Joshua at the camp at Makkedah. No one
dared to say anything negative about any soldier in the Israelite
army.

Joshua said, "Move the rocks that are covering the opening to that cave.
Bring to me those five kings out of that cave." So, Joshua's men
obeyed; they brought out those five kings from the cave—the
king of Jerusalem; the king of Hebron; the king of Jarmuth; the
king of Lachish; and the king of Eglon. When they brought out
those kings to Joshua, he summoned every one of his soldiers to
that spot. Joshua said to the military commanders who were
with him, "Come here! Put your feet on the necks of these
kings." (This was a symbolic action, expressing complete
victory.) So they got closer and put their feet on the necks of
those five kings.

Then Joshua said to his men, "Be strong and brave! Don't be afraid. I
will now show you what the Lord will do to the enemies whom
you will fight in the future." Then Joshua struck down the five
kings, executing them. Joshua hung up their corpses on five
trees. And he left them hanging on the trees until evening. At
sundown, Joshua commanded his men to take down the dead

bodies from the trees. Then the soldiers threw the corpses of the five kings into the same cave where they had been hiding. Then the soldiers closed up the opening to the cave with big rocks.

After this, Joshua and all Israel went back to the camp at Gilgal.

The Southern Cities Are Defeated

Next, Joshua captured Makkedah. He killed their king with a sword and completely destroyed all the people in that city; no one was left alive. Joshua did the same thing to the king of Makkedah as he had done to the king of Jericho. Then Joshua and all the Israelites moved on from Makkedah to Libnah. And they attacked Libnah. And the Lord handed over Libnah and its king to Israel. The army of Israel put everybody to the sword in the city of Libnah. None survived. So Joshua did the same thing to that king as he had done to the king of Jericho.

Then Joshua and all Israel moved on from Libnah to Lachish. They besieged Lachish, then attacked it. The Lord handed over Lachish to Israel. The Israelites captured it on the second day. They put everybody in there to the sword, just like Joshua had done to the city of Libnah. About this time, Horam the king of Gezer arrived to help defend the city of Lachish. So Joshua struck him down and also his army. None survived.

Then Joshua and all Israel moved on from Lachish to Eglon. They besieged Eglon and attacked it. They captured Eglon, using their swords to kill every single soul in Eglon; they completely destroyed everything. Then Joshua and all Israel went up from Eglon to Hebron and attacked it. They captured it and all of the villages near it. The Israelites put everybody in Hebron to the sword, including its king. (Because Joshua left no garrison to occupy and protect Hebron, the city had to be re-conquered later by Caleb [see Josh. 15:11-17].) None survived. They did the same thing that Joshua had done to the city of Eglon. They completely destroyed Hebron and every person in it. Then Joshua and all Israel went back to the city of Debir and attacked it. Next, Joshua captured Debir and its king, along with all of the villages near it. The Israelites struck them down with their swords. They completely destroyed everybody in Debir. None survived. Joshua did the same thing to Debir and its king that he had done to the city of Libnah and its king, and to the city of Hebron.

So Joshua defeated the entire country—the mountains, the Negev, the foothills, the slopes—and all of their kings. None survived. Joshua completely destroyed everything that breathed, just as the Lord, the God of Israel, had commanded. Joshua defeated all the cities from Kadesh-Barnea to Gaza. And he defeated all of the territory from Goshen to Gibeon. He captured all of those kings and their lands in a single campaign. (According to Unger, there were 25 city-states in Canaan when Israel entered it, and by 1390 B.C., Israel had swallowed up most of them. The Tel El-Amarna letters show that only four city-states were left.) Why? Because the Lord, the God of Israel, was fighting on behalf of Israel. Then Joshua and all Israel returned to their base camp at Gilgal.

The Sun Standing Still

The Lord said… "Do not fear them, for I have delivered them into your hand"…and he [Joshua] said in the sight of Israel: "Sun, stand still over Gibeon; and Moon, in the Valley of Aijalon" (Joshua 10:8,12).

Have you ever had problems because of a friend? Has the enemy ever tried to destroy you by attacking a friend of yours? That's what happened to Israel. God's people signed a peace pact with Gibeon, a neighboring tribe of people. The agreement said they would not fight each other, and if either of them were attacked, the one would come to the aid of the other (see Josh. 9:15). When five Amorite kings heard about the treaty, they attacked Gibeon. The Gibeonites quickly called for help from Joshua and the Israelites.

The Lord told Joshua, "I will give you victory over them" (Josh. 10:8 TLB). This was a great opportunity for Israel, they could get rid of five nations in one battle, but their opposition was five times larger than normal. So Joshua headed into battle with divine reassurance. Have you ever faced a spiritual battle with divine promises of victory, but you're still not sure what to do? Remember, sometimes God gives you victory by giving you inner strength. At other times, God does a miracle for you. God does what human effort can't do. Both of those things happened in this victory. *Lord, I want victory.*

First, Joshua made an all-night forced march across the mountains to catch the Amorites by surprise. Joshua's strategy and his army's physical conditioning gave Israel the upper hand at the beginning of the battle. When the Amorites retreated, Israel gave chase, killing them along the road. Remember the enemy slept the previous night, but not Israel. God's people were winning because they didn't give up. They didn't take time to rest. Maybe you need to learn tenacity. Don't give up and don't give in to your physical desires. *Lord, I will be strong.*

Then, God did two miracles to give them victory. First, "The Lord cast down large hailstones...There were more who died from the hailstones than the children of Israel killed with the sword" (Josh. 10:11.) Next, Joshua prayed for more sunlight to win the battle. He didn't want his enemy to reassemble or retreat into fortresses. Joshua called for a miracle, "...in the sight of Israel: 'Sun, stand still over Gibeon; and Moon, in the Valley of Aijalon.' So the sun stood still, and the moon stopped..." (Josh. 10:12-13.)

Just as God and Israel worked together for victory, so you have to walk with God for victory. The Living Bible describes it, "As God's partners" (2 Cor. 6:1.) *God, be my partner today.*

What does it mean to be a partner? It doesn't mean to quit working and let your partner do it all. Partnership means togetherness. Sometimes you begin a task, and the partner finishes up. So today you may have to take the first step toward victory. You may have to take the first spiritual step, as though you'll have to do everything yourself. Some battles Joshua fought without divine intervention. Joshua depended on the human ability of his soldiers. Sometimes you'll have to depend on others helping you, others like family or fellow workers. *Lord, send help.*

Sometimes the greatest help you get from a partner is encouragement and perhaps advice. Sometimes God will help you with biblical principles or strategy. When you follow the Bible's advice, you'll win the battle. At other times you'll be encouraged by "Christ in you the hope of glory" (Col. 1:27).

Let's not forget the physical aspect of victory. The soldiers had to march all night, then fight all day. That takes physical conditioning or stamina. Then the second night the sun didn't go down. Joshua prayed for the sun to stand still in the heavens. The soldiers didn't sleep the second night. There's a lesson here. Stay in good physical condition, you never know when a spiritual emergency will need all your strength to win a victory. Don't spend your nights seeking fun or spending your energy on frivolity. Remember, you must meet God each morning. God deserves your physical best. When you give your physical best to the lust of the flesh, then try to give some physical energy to God; you end up burning the candle on both ends. What glory does God get from your body, which is the temple of the Holy Spirit? Keep it in good physical condition. Some have been defeated spiritually, because they were tired physically. *Lord, I will discipline myself.*

Don't forget the role of prayer in victory. Notice what Joshua didn't pray about. He didn't ask for the battle to go away. Joshua asked God for *opportunity.* He asked God to give his army more daylight so they could continue fighting. Don't pray for the victory you're seeking, rather ask God to give you the *opportunity* to win the battle. You might pray for wisdom to handle the opposition, or wisdom to think up a workable plan.

You might ask God for friends to help you, for physical strength, or for circumstances. *Lord, give me the opportunity of victory.*

Get ready for your next spiritual battle. You may not be in one now, but it's coming. Jesus said, "In the world you will have tribulation; but be of good cheer, I have overcome the world" (John 16:33). *Lord, I'm getting ready.*

The Northern Cities Are Defeated

SCRIPTURE: JOSHUA 11

When Jabin (a dynasty title) the king of Hazor heard about what had happened, he sent urgent messages to Jobab the king of Madon; and to the king of Shimron; and to the king of Achshaph; and to the kings in the northern mountains; and to the kings in the Jordan Valley, south of Lake Galilee; and to the kings in the foothills and in Naphoth-Dor on the west. Jabin also sent word to the kings of the Canaanites in the east and in the west. He sent messages to the Amorites, the Hittites, the Perizzites, and the Jebusites in the hill-country. Jabin also sent word to the Hivites who lived below Mount Hermon and in the region of Mizpah. So these kings mobilized all their troops into a huge army, including a very large number of horses and chariots. In fact, it looked like there were as many men as the grains of sand at the seashore.

All of these kings met together at the waters of Merom. They consolidated their armies together into one camp and made plans to fight against the Israelites.

Then the Lord spoke to Joshua, "Don't be afraid of them. About this time tomorrow, I will hand all of them over to you dead—you will kill all of them. You must cripple the hind legs of their horses and set all of their chariots on fire." So Joshua and his entire army surprised that army. They attacked them beside the waters of Merom. (The Canaanite army was hemmed in between the mountains and Lake Merom. The horses and the charioteers had no time to deploy and no room to fight effectively. Undoubtedly, there was mass confusion because of Joshua's blitz.) So, the Lord did hand them over to the Israelites. They struck them down and chased them to greater Sidon (about 30 miles from the battlefield), to Misrephoth-Maim, and to the Valley of Mizpah in the east. The Israelites struck them until none of the Canaanites survived. Joshua did to them as the Lord told him. He crippled the hind legs of their horses and set their chariots on fire.

Then Joshua went back and captured the city of Hazor and executed its king. The city of Hazor had formally been the leader of all those kingdoms that fought against Israel. Israel killed everyone in Hazor, completely destroying them. Joshua did not leave anyone breathing. Then Joshua set the city of Hazor on fire, and executed all of their kings and captured all of the towns of those kings. Joshua completely destroyed them, just as Moses, the servant of the Lord, had commanded. However, except for the city of Hazor, the Israelites did not burn any cities that were built on their mounds (tels). Hazor was the only city that Joshua burned.

The people of Israel kept all the plunder of those towns for themselves. They seized all the animals, but they killed all the people there, until they were all destroyed. They left no one breathing. Previously, the Lord had commanded His servant Moses to do this. Then Moses commanded Joshua to do it. So Joshua carried out the punishment exactly as the Lord had commanded Moses.

So Joshua captured all of that land. He gained control of the mountains, all the Negev, all the Goshen region, the foothills, and the Jordan Valley, as well as the mountains of Israel and its foothills. Joshua controlled all the land from Mount Halak near Sier to Baal-Gad, in the valley of Lebanon, at the foot of Mount Hermon. Joshua captured all their kings and executed them. Joshua fought against all those kings for many years (seven years). Not a single city made peace with the Israelites, except the Hivites who lived in the city of Gibeon (they had a peace treaty). All the other cities were defeated in battle. Why? Because the Lord caused those people to be stubborn, so that they fought against Israel. In this way, the Lord could completely destroy them without mercy. That is what the Lord had commanded Moses to do.

Now at that time, Joshua went and wiped out the Anakites (a race of giants) who had come from the mountains of Hebron, of Debir, of Anab, and from all the hills of Judah and Israel. Joshua exterminated them and the Anakite towns. Joshua destroyed them so that there were no Anakites left living in the land of the Israelites. Only a few Anakites remained in Gaza, in Gath, and in Ashdod (Gath was the home of Goliath, the giant killed by David).

So Joshua took control of the entire country, just as the Lord had told Moses to do long ago. Joshua gave the land as an inheritance to Israel. Joshua divided up the land by their divisions and by their tribes. Then the land had rest; there was no more war. (No open Canaanite resistance, only some districts that were still not subdued [see Josh. 13:1-6].)

The Kings Defeated by Moses

SCRIPTURE: JOSHUA 12

The Israelites seized the land east of the Jordan River, from the Arnon
River to Mount Hermon, as well as all the land along the eastern
side of the Jordan Valley. These are the kings of the land whom they
struck down: Sihon was the king of the Amorites who lived in the
city of Heshbon and ruled the land from Aroer which is on the
banks of the Arnon River to the Jabbok River. His border started in
the middle of the river. It was the border of the Ammonites, that is
half of the land of Gilead. Sihon also ruled over the eastern side of
the Jordan Valley from Lake Galilee to the Jordan Valley Sea (also
called the Dead Sea). And Sihon ruled the land east of Beth-
Jeshimoth and south under the slopes of Pisgah. Then Israel
defeated Og, the king of Bashan who was one of the last of the
Rephaites. (A tribe of giants, like the Anakim.) He had lived in
Ashtaroth and in Edrei. Og had ruled over Mount Hermon, over
Salecah, and over all the region of Bashan. His land went to the
boundary of the people of Geshur and the people of Maacah. Og
had also ruled half of the land of Gilead, to the border of Sihon,
the king of Heshbon. Under the leadership of Moses, the Lord's
servant, the Israelites struck down both of those kings. And Moses,
the Lord's servant, gave that land as a possession to the tribe of
Reuben, the tribe of Gad, and to the half-tribe of Manasseh.

The Kings Defeated by Joshua

These are the kings of the land whom Joshua and the Israelites struck
down (the names of these kings were given in Joshua 12:9-27 in

the order that Joshua encountered them) west of the Jordan River. Then Joshua gave this land as a possession to the other tribes of Israel, according to their divisions. It was between Baal-Gad in the Valley of Lebanon and Mount Halak to Seir. This included the mountains, the foothills, and the Jordan Valley. It also included the eastern mountain slopes, the desert, and the Negev. This was the land where the Hittites, the Amorites, the Canaanites, the Perizzites, the Hivites and the Jebusites had lived.

They were one king of Jericho; one king of Ai which is near Bethel; one king of Jerusalem; one king of Hebron; one king of Jarmuth; one king of Lachish; one king of Eglon; one king of Gezer; one king of Debir; one king of Geder; one king of Hormah; one king of Arad; one king of Libnah; one king of Adullam; one king of Makkedah; one kind of Bethel; one king of Tappuah; one king of Hepher; one king of Aphek; one king of Lasharon; one king of Madon; one king of Hazor; one king of Shimron-Meron; one king of Achshaph; one king of Taanach; one king of Megiddo; one king of Kedesh; one king of Jokneam-in-Carmel; one king of Dor; one king of Goyim-in-Gilgal; and one king of Tirzah. The total number of kings was 31.

The Unconquered Land

SCRIPTURE: JOSHUA 13

When Joshua was very old (probably close to 100 years old; he died at
110 years of age [see Josh. 24:29]), the Lord spoke to him,
"Joshua, you are growing very old. Yet, much land still remains
to be conquered. These are the lands which still remain unconquered: all the areas of the Philistines; and, all the territory of
the people of Geshur from the Shihor River which faces Egypt;
and, to the border of Ekron northward—that is regarded as
"Canaanite." You must defeat the five Philistine rulers. They are
at Gaza, at Ashdod, at Ashkelon, at Gath, and at Ekron. You
must also defeat the Avvites, on the south, all the land of the
Canaanites; and Mearah, which belongs to the Sidonians; to
Aphek; to the border of the Amorites; and the land of the
Gebalites; and all Lebanon, toward the east, from Baal-Gad at
the foot of Mount Hermon to Lebo-Hamath; and all those who
live in the hill-country, from Lebanon to Misrephoth-Maim,
including all the Sidonians. Nevertheless, I Myself will force
them out ahead of the Israelites. Just be sure to divide up the
land to Israel as an inheritance, as I have commanded you. So
now divide up this land as an inheritance among the nine tribes
and the western half-tribe of Manasseh."

Dividing the Land That Was East of the Jordan River

Along with the eastern half-tribe of Manasseh, the tribes of Reuben and
Gad had previously received their land-inheritance that Moses
gave them east of the Jordan River. The following is what Moses,

the servant of the Lord, gave to them: their land began from
Aroer, which is on the edge of the Arnon Ravine, and went to
the town in the middle of the ravine, and it included the whole
tableland from Medeba to Dibon. All the towns that Sihon the
king of the Amorites had ruled while in the city of Heshbon
were on that land. The land continued to the border of the
Ammonites; and to Gilead; and to the border of the Geshurites;
and to the border of the Maachathites; and all of Mount
Hermon; and all of Bashan, as far as Salecah; to all of the kingdom of Og, the king of Bashan, who had ruled at Ashtaroth and
at Edrei. Previously, Moses had struck them down and had
forced them out. However, the Israelites did not force out the
people of Geshur and the people of Maacah. They still live
among the Israelites today (at the time the Book of Joshua was
written).

The tribe of Levi was the only tribe that did not receive any land-
inheritance. Instead, they were to be given all the fire offerings
which were sacrificed to the Lord, the God of Israel. That is their
inheritance, just as God said to them.

Moses had given each clan from the tribe of Reuben some land: their
border was from Aroer, which is at the edge of the Arnon
Ravine, including the city which is in the middle of the ravine,
extending from all of the tableland around the town of Medeba.
The land reached to Heshbon; and all of its towns which are on
the tableland—Dibon; Bamoth-Baal; and Beth-Baal-Meon;
Jahaz; Kedemoth; Mephaath; Kiriathaim; Sibmah; Zereth-Shahar
on the hill of the valley; Beth-Peor; the slopes of Pisgah; Beth-
Jeshimoth; that is, all of the towns of the tableland; and all of
the kingdom of Sihon, the king of the Amorites, who had ruled
in the city of Heshbon. But Moses struck Sihon down, as well as
the sheiks of Midian—Evi, Rekem, Zur, Hur, and Reba—
chieftains of Sihon who lived in the land. The Israelites killed

many people with swords, including Balaam, the son of Beor,
the fortune-teller (see Num. 22:1-25; 31:16, Mic. 6:5, 2 Peter
2:15-16). The territory of the Reubenites had the Jordan River as
the boundary. This was the land-inheritance of the Reubenites,
according to their clans, with their towns and villages.

And Moses gave a land-inheritance to the tribe of Gad, to the sons of
Gad, according to their clans. Their territory was Jazer, and all
the towns of Gilead, and half of the land of the Ammonites, to
Aroer, which is near Rabbah. And it included that area from
Heshbon to Ramath-Mizpeh and Betonim; from Mahanaim to
the territory of Debir; in the valley of Beth-ha-Ram; Beth-
Nimrah; Succoth; Zaphon; and all the rest of the kingdom of
Sihon, the king of Heshbon; the Jordan River and its boundary
line; to the edge of Lake Galilee; east of the Jordan River. This
was the land-inheritance of the sons of Gad, according to their
clans, towns, and villages.

And Moses gave an inheritance to the eastern half-tribe of Manasseh. It
was allotted to the half-tribe of Manasseh, according to their
clans. Their territory began at Mahanaim. It included all of
Bashan; all the kingdom of Og, the king of Bashan; all the small
towns of Jair, which are in Bashan (60 towns); half of Gilead;
the city of Ashtaroth and the city of Edrei. These were royal
cities of Og in Bashan. All of this land was given to the family of
Machir, the son of Manasseh. Half of Machir's sons had been
given this land by their clans.

These are the ones to whom Moses gave this land-inheritance, when
Moses was on the tableland of Moab. It was east of the Jordan
River, just across from the city of Jericho.

However, Moses did not give any land-inheritance to the tribe of Levi.
The Lord Himself, the God of Israel, is their inheritance, just as
He promised them.

The Division of Canaan

SCRIPTURE: JOSHUA 14

Eleazar the high priest, Joshua the son of Nun, and all the leaders of the
tribes of the Israelite people decided on what inheritances in the
land of Canaan to distribute to the Israelites. They picked lots to
decide which lands they would receive. Previously, through
Moses, the Lord had commanded how He wanted the nine and
a half tribes to inherit their land. Moses had already distributed
to the two and a half tribes their land-inheritances east of the
Jordan River. However, the tribe of Levi did not receive any land-
inheritance among them. Except for some towns in which to live
and the pasturelands for their livestock and property, the Levites
did not receive a portion in the land of Canaan. The sons of
Joseph became two tribes—Manasseh and Ephraim. (See
Genesis 48:5. Because of Reuben's incest with Bilhah [see Gen.
35:22], Joseph was awarded the double portion inheritance that
usually went to the firstborn son, Reuben.) The Lord had commanded Moses how to divide up the land to the Israelites. And
that's the way they did it. (Though surveying and measuring
would take considerable time to do.) *Lord, thank You for prede-
termining where each tribe would be located. If You had not made
the choice for each, they probably would have argued over the
land.*

Caleb's Inheritance

Some men from the tribe of Judah came near Joshua in Gilgal. (Note:
Before the intended allotment for the tribe of Judah was set,

PRAYING WITH THE CONQUERORS

Caleb wanted to make sure that his prior claim was honored.) One of those men was Caleb, the son of Jephunneh the Kenizzite. Caleb said to Joshua, "Do you remember what the Lord said at Kadesh-Barnea speaking to Moses, the man of God, about you and me? Moses, the Lord's servant, sent me from Kadesh-Barnea to spy on the land of Canaan. I was 40 years old then. When I came back, I told Moses what I thought about the land. But ten other Hebrew brothers who went up with me told the people things that made them afraid. But I fully believed that the Lord would empower us to capture the land. So on that day, Moses vowed: 'The land where you went will surely become your land. You and your descendants will always own it, because you wholly followed after the Lord our God.'" *Lord, Heaven is my "land-inheritance."*

"And now, look, the Lord has kept me alive—just as He promised—for the past 45 years, (after the return of the 12 spies in the autumn of the second year following the exodus [see Num. 13:25], 38 years transpired until the nation of Israel reached the Jordan River [see Num. 20:1]. Therefore, Caleb is staking his claim seven years into Joshua's military campaigns to conquer Palestine) since the Lord made that statement to Moses. During that time, we crisscrossed the desert. And now, look, I am 85 years old today. I am just as strong as I was on that day when Moses sent me out. I am also just as ready to fight now as I was then. I can still get around just fine. So now, give me this mountain (this highland region) which the Lord promised me on that day long ago. Back then, you heard that the Anakites (a race of giants) lived there, and that the cities were large and well-protected. But now, with the Lord's help, I will force those people out, (though Joshua's initial campaigns into southern Canaan had previously expelled the Anakites, they only withdrew temporarily to Philistine territory. Then the Anakites recaptured and reoccupied Hebron) just as the Lord has said." *Lord, remind me that one sin over a sin doesn't guarantee future victory on a continued basis. Life is a continual struggle against sin.*

So Joshua blessed Caleb, the son of Jephunneh, and allotted to him the city of Hebron for his land-inheritance. Therefore, Hebron still belongs to the family of Caleb the son of Jephunneh, the Kenizzite, until this very day, because Caleb completely followed after the Lord, the God of Israel. In the past, Hebron was named "Kiriath-Arba," after a great hero among the Anakites. Then there was peace in the land. *Lord, may I be faithful to You to the end of my life as was Caleb.*

Caleb's Mountain

And Caleb...said..."I was forty years old when...the Lord sent me...to spy out the land...I wholly followed the Lord my God. Now, behold the Lord has kept me alive...these forty-five years...I am as strong this day as on the day that Moses sent me...now therefore, give me this mountain" (Joshua 14:6-8,10-12).

It is said that dreams keep us alive. And if we have no dreams, we might as well be dead, even though we're still alive. Today, what dreams give you a desire to get up in the morning? What dreams drive you to meaningful work? What dreams compel you to make a contribution to life? *Lord, help me see Your dream for my life.*

Now, Caleb was 85 years of age and still wanted his mountain. Forty years earlier Caleb surveyed the Promised Land as a spy; that's when he saw Hebron. When he asked for it, Moses said he could have it. Has God shown you something you want? Do you have faith to believe God would give your mountain to you? *Lord, there is a mountain I want.*

In today's story, it's 45 years later, and Caleb still dreams about his mountain. After wandering in the wilderness 40 years, and after fighting five years for other sections of the Promised Land, Caleb is ready to claim his mountain.

There are at least four steps to receiving your dream.

First, you must *see the mountain*. Peter said, "Your young men shall see visions, your old men shall dream dreams" (Acts 2:17). A *vision* is off in the future, it's what the young desire to have. *Dreams* are past events that you haven't realized, but you still strive to accomplish. Hebron was the tallest mountain in the region. And if you lived on Hebron, you could look down on everything that looks up to you. As a young man, Caleb had a *vision* of building a home there; now as an old man, the *dream* has not yet happened. Do you have a dream that hasn't yet materialized? *Lord, I have a dream!*

Second, you must ask. This means asking God and asking people. "You do not have because you do not ask" (James 4:2.) You've got to know when to ask, what to ask, how to ask, and who to ask. Are you ready to ask for your dream? *Lord, give me my dream.*

The third step is committing yourself to work and/or fight for your dream. Caleb asked for a mountain filled with the enemy. He didn't ask Joshua to fight for him nor did he ask the army to get it for him. Caleb didn't use his position to ask for exemptions or privileges. He asked for the opportunity to fight/work for the mountain promised to him. *Lord, I am willing to work/fight for my dream.*

Finally, Caleb trusted God to help him victoriously conquer the mountain, "It may be that the Lord will be with me, and I shall be able to drive them out" (Josh. 14:12). It's one thing to have a dream, but a dream is only the beginning. It's another step forward when you pray and work for your dream. But what about victory? How do you capture your dream? It takes God and man working together. By faith you have to work hard and work smart. And as you work for your dream, you have to know how to work with God. *Lord, I'm working, help me.*

How long have you been waiting for your dream? Caleb had to wait 45 years. That's a long time in anyone's life. Have you noticed that a burning desire to achieve a dream goes along with patient endurance to wait for a dream? Young people have the burning desire to achieve a dream. But most of them want their mountain *now!* And if they don't get their dream within a short period of time, they give up. Or they get a new dream. Many young people lack patience. It's easier for elderly people to have patience, even if they don't have much time left in life. What's strongest for you, burning desire or patience? *Lord, mix perfectly my dream and my patience to get my mountain-dream.*

There's another principle you need to know about getting your mountain— timing. You have to know when to wait and when to act. If you act too soon, you might not get your dream because the circumstances are not right. And if you act too early, you may spoil any chances of ever getting your dream at a later time. If you have only one bullet in your gun, and you shoot too soon; you have nothing to shoot when you face an emergency. *God, teach me how to wait for the perfect time to act on getting my mountain.*

Some people let the perfect time come and go; they do nothing. If you have only one bullet in your gun, and you don't shoot when your life is threatened, later it may be impossible to pull the trigger. You may be dead. Some people die because all they've done is wait for an opportunity to conquer their mountain. When a door opens, you must walk through; it may not open again. *Lord, teach me perfect timing.*

Blessed are the unsatisfied when they have a dream, for they have a reason to live. Do you have a life-motivating dream? Better than money, position, and friends, a dream may be your best possession in life. For when you have a dream, you have a reason to live. And a life with purpose, is the best life possible. "For to me, to live is Christ, and to die is gain" (Phil. 1:21.) *Lord, give me a dream and accomplish my dream in my lifetime.*

Dividing Up the Promised Land

SCRIPTURE: JOSHUA 15

The property that was assigned was by lot (probably two small stones
[possibly one white and one black] were placed in the pocket of
the High Priest's vest [breast plate]. Prayer was made to commit
the decision to God. So lots were a very serious business. It
meant that the participant was seeking God's will in making a
major decision [see Prov. 16:33]) for the tribe of the people of
Judah; for their clans including southward to the border of
Edom, to the desert of Zin at the extreme south. And their
southern border ran from the end of the Dead Sea, from the bay
that faces southward. It goes out southward of the Ascent of
Akrabbim, passing along to Zin. Then it goes up to the south of
Kadesh-Barnea, along by Hezron, and up to Addar, where it
turns toward Karka. It continues to Azmon, going out by the
Brook of Egypt, and comes to its end at the Mediterranean Sea.
This will be the southern border. *Lord, thank You for guiding
Your people by lots. Today I shall find Your will in Scripture.*

And the eastern border is the Dead Sea, at the end of the Jordan River.
And the border on the north side runs from the bay of the Dead
Sea, at the end of the Jordan River. Then the border went up to
Beth-Hoglah, and it continued north of Beth-Arabah. Then the
border went on up to the Stone of Bohan. (Bohan was the son
of Reuben.) And the border goes on up to Debir from the Valley
of Achor, and so on northward, turning toward Gilgal, which is
opposite the Ascent of Adummim, which is on the south side of
the valley. Then the border passes along to the waters of En-
Shemesh, and it stops at En-Rogel. Then the border goes up the

Valley of Ben-Hinnom, which is next to the southern side of the
Jebusite city. (That is now called Jerusalem.) There the border
goes up to the top of the mountain, which is on the west side of
Hinnom Valley, at the northern end of the Valley of Rephaim.
Then the border extends from the top of the mountain to the
spring of the Waters of Nephtoah. Then it goes to the towns
near Mount Ephron. Then the border bends around to Baalah
(that is Kiriath-Jearim). At Baalah, the border turned west and
goes toward Mount Seir. It passes along the north side of Mount
Jearim (that is, Chesalon) and goes down the Beth-Shemesh.
From there it goes along past Timnah. Then the border goes out
to the northern slope of Ekron. Then the border bends around
toward Shikkeron and extends to Mount Baalah, where it goes
out to Jabneel. The border ends at the Mediterranean Sea.

And the western border was the Mediterranean Sea, with its coastline.

This is the border all around the people of Judah, according to their
clans.

The Lord had commanded Joshua to give Caleb part of the land among
the people of Judah. So Joshua gave that land to Caleb. He gave
him the town of Kiriath-Arba, that is, Hebron. Caleb forced out
the three Anakite families living in Hebron. They were descendants of Sheshai, Ahiman, and Talmai, the sons of Anak. Then
Caleb fought against the people living in Debir previously called
Kiriath-Sepher. Then Caleb said, "I want a man to attack and
capture Kiriath-Sepher. I will give him Achsah, my daughter, for
a wife." Othniel (see Judg. 1:13; 3:9) the descendant of Kenaz
(the brother of Caleb) captured the city. So Caleb gave his
daughter Achsah to Othniel to be his wife. Achsah went and
urged Othniel to ask her father Caleb for more land. But when
Achsah got off her donkey, Caleb asked her, "What do you
want?" Achsah answered, "I would like a special favor. Since you
have given me land in the Negev (desert), give me also springs

of water." So Caleb gave her the upper springs and the lower springs. *Lord, teach me to ask (pray) for necessities.*

The following is the land-inheritance of the tribe of the people of Judah, according to their clans. The towns which belonged to the tribe of the people of Judah in the Negev, toward the border of Edom, were: Kabzeel; Eder; Jagur; Kinah; Dimonah; Adadah; Kedesh; Hazor; Ithnan; Ziph; Telem; Bealoth; Hazor-Hadattah; Kerioth-Hezron (that is Hazor); Amam; Shema; Moladah; Hazar-Gaddah; Heshmon; Beth-Pelet; Hazar-Shual; Beer-Sheba; Biziothiah; Baalah; Iim; Ezem; Elotlad; Kesil; Hormah; Ziklag; Madmannah; Sansannah; Lebaoth; Shilhim; Ain; and Rimmon. There were a total of 29 towns, along with their villages.

The tribe of Judah received these following towns in the foothills: Eshtaol; Zorah; Ashnah; Zanoah; En-Gannim; Tappuah; Enam; Jarmuth; Adullam; Socoh; Azekah; Shaaraim; Adithaim; Gederah (also called Gederothaim). There were 14 towns, along with their villages.

The tribe of Judah also received these towns in the foothills: Zenan; Hadashah; Migdal-Gad; Dilean; Mizpah; Joktheel; Lachish; Bozkath; Eglon; Cabbon; Lahmas; Kitlish; Gederoth; Beth-Dagon; Naamah; and Makkedah. There were 16 towns, along with their villages.

The tribe of Judah also received these following towns in the foothills: Libnah; Ether; Ashan; Iphtah; Ashnah; Nezib; Keilah; Achzib; and Mareshah. These were nine towns, along with their villages.

The tribe of Judah also received the city of Ekron, along with its surrounding settlements and villages from Ekron to the Mediterranean Sea—everything that was next to Ashdod, along with its villages; the city of Ashdod, along with its surrounding settlements and its villages; the city of Gaza, along with its surrounding settlements and its villages; to the Brook of Egypt, and the Mediterranean Sea and its coastline.

The tribe of Judah also received these following towns in the mountains: Shamir; Jattir; Socoh; Dannah; Kiriath-Sannah (that is Debir); Anab; Eshtemoh; Anim; Goshen; Holon; and Giloh. There were 11 towns, along with their villages.

The tribe of Judah also received these following towns in the mountains: Arab; Dumah; Eshan; Janim; Beth-Tappuah; Aphekah; Humtah; Kiriath-Arba (that is, Hebron); and Zior. There were nine towns, along with their villages.

The tribe of Judah also received these following towns in the mountains: Maon; Carmel; Ziph; Juttah; Jezreel; Jokdeam; Zanoah; Kain; Gibeah; and Timnah. There were ten towns, along with their villages.

The tribe of Judah also received these following towns in the mountains: Halhul; Beth-Zur; Gedor; Maarath; Beth-Anoth; and Eltekon. There were six towns, along with their villages.

The tribe of Judah also received the two towns of Rabbah and Kiriath-Baal (that is Kiriath-Jearim), along with their villages.

The tribe of Judah also received some towns in the desert: Beth-Arabah; Middin; Secacah; Nibshan; the City of Salt; and En-Gedi. There were six towns, along with their villages.

The army of Judah was not able to force out the Jebusites (the ones who lived in Jerusalem). So the Jebusites still live among the people of Judah in Jerusalem to this day (at the time the Book of Joshua was written). *Lord, remind me that an incomplete victory is also a commitment to future struggle with that same problem.*

Ephraim and Manasseh's Share

SCRIPTURE: JOSHUA 16

The property that was assigned by lot to the sons of Joseph (Manasseh and Ephraim) was received. It went out from the Jordan River near Jericho. And it continued to the waters of Jericho, eastward, toward the desert, which went up from Jericho to the hills of Bethel. Then it went out from Bethel to Luz, passing along to the border of the Archites to Ataroth. Then it went down west to the border of the Japhletites. And it continued to the border of Lower Beth-Horon, and on to Gezer. The border ended at the Mediterranean Sea.

So Manasseh and Ephraim inherited their land. *Lord, thank You for remembering the good things Joseph did for You.*

The territory of the Ephraimites, by their clans was this: The border of their land-inheritance started at Ataroth-Addar on the east. It went as far as Upper Beth-Horon. Then the border extended to the sea. Michmethath is on the north. Then, on the east, the border turns around toward Taanath-Shiloh and passes along beyond it to the Janoah on the east. Then it goes down from Janoah to Ataroth and to Naarah. It continues until it touches Jericho and stops at the Jordan River. The border goes west from Tappuah to Kanah Ravine. And the Mediterranean Sea is the boundary. This is all the land-inheritance of the tribe of the Ephraimites, by their clans, including the towns which were set aside for the Ephraimites inside the land-inheritance of the Manassites—all those towns, as well as their villages. But the Ephraimites could not force the Canaanites to leave Gezer. So the Canaanites still live among the Ephraimites today (at the time the Book of Joshua was written). But they became slaves of the Ephraimites, doing forced labor. (The Israelites did not obey God's command in Deuteronomy 20:16-18.)

Property and Territories Given Out

Scripture: Joshua 17

The property that was assigned by lot for the half-tribe of Manasseh
was received. (He was Joseph's firstborn.) Manasseh's firstborn
was Machir, the father of Gilead. The Machirites were great soldiers. So the region of Gilead and Bashan was given to them.
The allotments were made to the rest of the descendants of the
half-tribe of Manasseh, by their clans: for the sons of Abiezer, for
the sons of Helek, for the sons of Asriel, for the sons of
Shechem, for the sons of Hepher, and for the sons of Shemida.
These were all the male descendants of Manasseh the sons of
Joseph, by their clans.

Now Zelophehad was the son of Hepher, the grandson of Gilead, the
great-grandson of Machir, and the great-great-grandson of
Manasseh. But Zelophehad himself had no sons—only daughters. The names of his daughters were: Mahlah, Noah, Hoglah,
Milcah, and Tirzah. These daughters went into the presence of
Eleazar, the high priest. They also went to Joshua the son of Nun
and all the leaders. They said, "The Lord commanded Moses to
give us daughters a land-inheritance, the same as our Hebrew
male relatives." So, Eleazar obeyed the Lord—he gave the daughters of Zelophehad their land-inheritance, just like Zelophehad's
male relatives received. So, the half-tribe of Manasseh got ten
sections of land, in addition to the land of Gilead and Bashan,
which was east of the Jordan River. The female descendants of
Manasseh also received land-inheritances, just like the men did.
The land of Gilead was allotted to the rest of the descendants of
Manasseh.

The border of Manasseh reaches from Asher to Michmethath, which is
east of Shechem. Then the border goes south to where the people of En-Tappuah live. The land of Tappuah belonged to the
tribe of Manasseh, but the town of Tappuah on the boundary-
line of Manasseh belonged to the Ephraimites. The border of
Manasseh goes down to Kanah Ravine, south of the creek.
These towns of the half-tribe of Ephraim were interlaced among
the towns of the half-tribe of Manasseh. Then the border of
Manasseh goes on the north side of the creek, and it ends at the
Mediterranean Sea. The land toward the south belongs to
Ephraim. And the land toward the north belongs to Manasseh.
The sea is the western boundary line. And the border touches
the territory of the tribe of Asher on the north. And it touches
the land of the tribe of Issachar on the east.

In addition, in the territories of Issachar and Asher, the people
Manasseh had the rights to Beth-Shean and its villages; to
Ibleam and its villages; to those who lived in Dor and its villages; to those who lived in En-Dor and its villages; to those
who lived in Taanach and its villages; and to those who lived in
Megiddo and its villages—three districts. However, Manasseh
was not able to force out the local people of those cities because
the Canaanites were determined to keep on living in this land.
But when the Israelites grew strong, they forced the Canaanites
to work for them. But the Israelites never did force them to completely leave the land.

Now, the people from the tribes of Joseph spoke to Joshua. They said,
"You gave us as an inheritance only one area of land and one
share of the land, yet we are so numerous. (This was an unwar-
ranted, unreasonable complaint. They were exaggerating; they
were not much more numerous than the single tribe of Judah
[see Num. 26:22=76,500]. And half of them had already been

settled on the east side of the Jordan River.) Up until now, the Lord has blessed us abundantly."

And Joshua answered them, "Since you do have so many people, go up to the forest. Clear a place for yourselves to live there. That is in the land of the Perizzites and the Rephaites, if the hill-country of Ephraim is too small for you!" *Lord, just as Joshua let the people determine their own future and inheritance, You do the same for me today.*

The people of Joseph said, "It's true. The hill-country of Ephraim is not big enough for us, but the areas where the Canaanites live in the plains are dangerous, those in Beth-Shean and its villages and those in the Valley of Jezreel—they've got iron chariots." *Lord, I will not look at the might of my enemies, but I'll look to Your strength.*

Then Joshua spoke to the people of Joseph—to Ephraim and to Manasseh. He said, "There are so many of you, and you do have great power. You should not be given more than one share of the land. (Not being intimidated, Joshua corrected them: It is not "one lot only." This one huge plain of Esdraelon [12 miles × 16 miles] assigned to them already included all that territory in the hill-country and the vast forest that should have been cleared.) Of course, you are a great people. Get up and prove it by driving out those Canaanites. The hill-country also belongs to you. Even though it is now a forest, you can cut down the trees and it will be yours. And you will possess all of it, because you will force the Canaanites out of the land. You *can* defeat them, even though they have iron chariots and they are strong." *Lord, have faith in me to win a victory, just as Joshua had faith in the people to be victorious.*

Driving Out the Canaanites

You should drive out the Canaanites, though they have iron chariots and though they are strong (Joshua 17:18).

Just because Israel entered the Promised Land by miraculously crossing the Jordan River does not guarantee they will easily possess the land. No! Israel had to fight to possess its land. In the same way, just because you were miraculously born again in conversion does not guarantee you will be a victorious Christian. The Christian life will be a fight against your original sin nature, and a struggle against deceptive temptations. Sin is powerful. Satan is insidious. The flesh clamors for satisfaction, and the world will constantly entice you. *Lord, I'll lose if You don't help me.*

Many have wrongly pictured crossing Jordan as a picture of death. No, crossing Jordan does not represent death, because Israel crossed over on dry land—an easy crossing. Most die in pain, with shriveled bodies, and debilitating diseases. And they wrongly describe Canaan as Heaven. But Heaven is peace, contentment, and worship. Israel struggled to conquer giants, fortified cities, and they struggled with their own inner sin, the treachery of Achan's lust for things. *Lord, I want to be victorious over sin, so I will struggle on.*

Notice the command, "You shall drive them out." You must drive out every enemy, though they are strong. Whether that enemy is alcohol, gossiping, or hatred; you must win every battle, just as Israel had to drive out the enemy to possess their land-inheritance. You cannot pray to ask God to drive them out for you. No! You must fight against sin...all kinds of sin...every last bit of sin. Don't make friends with your enemy; don't allow them to remain in your life. You cannot be a victorious believer by friendship with evil, just as Eve sinned after she became a friend of the serpent. Sin will utterly destroy your soul, as the serpent delivered death to Eve. *Lord, give me eyes to see evil, and conviction to overcome it.*

Israel didn't have chariots or horses, but the Canaanites did. They were a fierce people and their chariots had iron wheels. An army without chariots drug out logs before charging chariots to break the chariot wheels—

but iron wheels could fly over any barrier and crush the arms and legs of defenseless soldiers. In like picture, our spiritual enemy has "iron wheels." Our enemy—the world, the flesh, and the devil—can fly over any defense we drag out against sin. We can't stand alone against the brilliance of satan. But He who fights on our side is God. The Lord will fight with us, for us, and in us. "Greater is He who is in you, than he who is in the world." *Lord, I rely on You for victory.*

Look again at the command, "You shall drive out the Canaanites." This simple declarative sentence encompasses all of the Canaanites. "Drive them out." Don't leave even a "little one" in the land. God had given up the Canaanites (Rom. 1:24,26,28) because of their infectious sexual sins, their homosexuality, their rebellion against righteousness, their envy, murder, deceit, pride, and lying ways. God didn't want them to corrupt His people. "Don't give your daughters to marry them and don't let your sons marry their daughters." Total separation. Total abandonment of sin. *Lord, help me when I'm tempted, and I will stand for You.*

Because of the Canaanite war against Israel, apply this truth to your life. Sin wars against you. Watch out...pull your sword...fight...don't look back...don't think of running away. If you let the smallest sin live in your heart, it will begin conquering you all over again. Remember, "He who knew no sin was made sin for you." From our sins came the crown of thorns, the whip, the nails, the spear, and death itself. He suffered and died for your sins. *Lord, the blood of Jesus Christ Your Son cleanses me from every sin.*

You cannot say, "I can't help it," or, "I didn't know what I was doing," or, "Sin is so natural." You *can* help it, and you *do* know what you are doing, and sin is not natural to the new nature. Yes, iron chariot wheels attack suddenly when you're not prepared, and yes, iron chariot wheels seem to stop at nothing. But you're different from other peoples; you're a child of God. You have a new nature that points out right from wrong. You have been transformed by Christ. Victory is possible if you want it. Yield to God's strength, "For we are workmen together with Christ." *Lord, when I'm weak, I need Your strength. When I'm blinded to sin, I need Your illumination. When I'm attacked, I need Your victory.*

The Rest of the Land Is Divided

SCRIPTURE: JOSHUA 18

The Israelite community gathered together at Shiloh. (Probably exclud-
ing the tribes of Judah, Ephraim, Manasseh, Reuben, and Gad
because those tribes had already received allotments. This site
was determined by Joshua under divine direction [see Deut.
12:11]. The Tabernacle remained at Shiloh for more than 300
years [see 1 Sam. 4:1-11]). There they set up the Tabernacle. The
Israelites had control of that land, but there were still seven
tribes of the Israelites that had not yet shared in the land-
inheritances. *Lord, You didn't overlook any, so don't overlook me.*

So Joshua said to the Israelites: "Why do you wait so long to capture
your land? (Apparently, the remaining Israelites became too satisfied with the fertile districts where they were, instead of contin-
uing the conquest.) The Lord, the God of your ancestors, has
given this land to you. Each tribe must choose three men. (A
total of 21 highly-qualified surveyors.) I will send them off to
map out the territory. They will write a description of it, so that I
can divide up your land-inheritances. Then they will come back
to report to me. Then we will divide up the land into seven
parts. The people of Judah will stay within their borders in the
south. The people of Joseph will stay within their borders in the
north. However, you will divide the land into seven parts.
Describe the seven parts in writing. Then bring what you have
written here to me. We will let the Lord our God pick the lots.
(In the presence of Yahweh, our God, He will decide which tribe
will get what land.) But the Levites do not get any part of these
lands, because the priesthood of the Lord is their inheritance.

Gad, Reuben, and the eastern half-tribe of Manasseh already have received their land-inheritance on the east side of the Jordan River. Moses, the servant of the Lord gave it to them." *Lord, thank You for being fair.*

So the men who were selected went into the countryside. The plan was for them to describe it in writing and take it back to Joshua. Joshua directed them: "Go and survey the land, map it out in writing and come back to me. Then I will ask the Lord to choose which land you should receive here at Shiloh." So the men left and passed throughout the countryside, mapping it town-by-town in a book for Joshua. It had seven sections. Then they returned to Joshua who was at the camp in Shiloh. Then in the presence of the Lord, Joshua picked lots for them to apportion the land that should be distributed to each tribe, according to their divisions. *Lord, thank You for using human people to carry out Your will. Use me also.*

Benjamin's Share

The first property that was assigned by lot for the tribe of the sons of Benjamin was received, according to their clans. The boundary line of Benjamin's lot goes out between the territory of the sons of Judah and the territory of the sons of Joseph. The northern border starts at the Jordan River, going along the northern boundary of the city of Jericho. Then it goes west into the mountains, extending to the desert of Beth-Aven. From there, the border goes south to Luz (that is Bethel), at the edge of town. Then it goes down to Ataroth-Addar, which is on the hill that lies south of lower Beth-Horon. Then the border goes in another direction, turning on the western side southward from the mountain which faces the south, opposite Beth-Horon. And its boundary line ends at Kiriath-Baal (that is, Kiriath-Jearim), a town that belongs to the tribe of Judah. This forms the western side.

Now the southern side starts at the outskirts of Kiriath-Jearim. Then the border goes west from there to the spring of the waters of Nephtoah. Then the border goes down to the bottom of the mountain, that is near the valley of Ben-Hinnom, which is north, in the valley of Rephaim. The border goes down the Hinnom Valley, just south of the Jebusite city (Jerusalem) and on down to En-Rogel. Then the border goes in another direction; it turns north and goes out to En-Shemesh. Then it goes on out to Geliloth, which is opposite the Ascent of Adummim. Then it goes down to the Stone of Bohan. (Bohan was the son of Reuben.) Passing on to the north side of Beth-Arabah, the border goes on down to the Jordan Valley. Then the border passes on to the north side of Beth-Hoglah. It comes out at the north bay of the Dead Sea. This is where the Jordan River flows into the sea. This is the southern border.

The Jordan River forms the boundary on the east side. So, this was the land-inheritance that was distributed to the sons of Benjamin, according to their clans. These were the borders on all sides.

Now the towns of the tribe of the sons of Benjamin, according to their clans, were: Jericho; Beth-Hoglah; Emek-Keziz; Beth-Arabah; Zemaraim; Bethel; Avvim; Parah; Ophrah; Chephar-Ammoni; Ophni; and Geba. There were 12 towns, along with their villages.

The tribe of Benjamin also possessed these towns: Gibeon; Ramah; Beeroth; Mizpeh; Chephirah; Mozah; Rekem; Irpeel; Taralah; Zela; Ha-Eleph; Jebus (that is Jerusalem); Gibeah; and Kiriath. There were 14 towns, along with its villages. This is the land-inheritance of the tribe of Benjamin, according to its clans. *Lord, You are gracious.*

Simeon's Share

SCRIPTURE: JOSHUA 19

The second property that was assigned by the lot of the tribe of Simeon
was received, according to their clans. Their inheritance was
located within the land of the sons of Judah.

They received these towns; Beer-Sheba; Sheba; Moladah; Hazar-Shual;
Balah; Ezem; Eltolad; Bethul; Hormah; Ziklag; Beth-Marcaboth;
Hazar-Susah; Beth-Lebaoth; and Sharuhen. There were
13 towns, along with their villages.

They also received the towns of: Ain; Rimmom; Ether; and Ashan.
There were four towns, along with their villages, including all
the villages that were surrounding these towns as far as Baalath-
Beer. (This is the same as Ramah-Negev.)

So this is the land-inheritance distributed to the tribe of the sons of
Simeon, clan-by-clan.

The Simeonites' land-inheritance was taken from part of the territory of
Judah, because the sons of Judah had more land than they could
use. So the Simeonites received their own land-inheritance within
the land of Judah.

Zebulun's Share

The third property that was assigned by the lot for the tribe of Zebulun
was received, according to their clans. The border of their land-
inheritance was as far as Sarid. Then it goes up west to Maralah
and it touches Dabbesheth. Then it reaches the ravine near

Jokneam and it turns back from Sarid eastward, to the boundary line of Chisloth-Tabor. Then it goes out to Daberath and goes up to Japhia. From there, it passes along east to Gath-Hepher and to Eth-Kazin. Then it extends to Rimmon, bending toward Neah. Then on the north, the border turns around to Hannathon, and it ends at the valley of Iphtah-El. These were some other towns inside this border: Kattath; Nahalal; Shimron; Idalah; and Bethlehem. There were 12 towns, along with their villages. This is the land-inheritance of the tribe of Zebulun, according to their clans—these towns, along with their villages.

Issachar's Share

The fourth property that was assigned by the lot for the tribe of Issachar was received, according to their clans. Their territory included: Jezreel; Chesulloth; Shunem; Hapharaim; Shion; Anaharath; Rabbith; Kishion; Ebez; Remeth; En-Gannim; En-Haddah; and Beth-Pazzez. The border also touches Tabor, Shahazumah, and Beth-Shemesh. It stops at the Jordan River. There were 16 towns, along with their villages. This is the land-inheritance of the tribe of the sons of Issachar, according to their clans, towns, and villages.

Asher's Share

The fifth property that was assigned by the lot for the tribe of the sons of Asher was received, according to their clans. Their territory included: Helkath; Hali; Beten; Achshaph; Allammelech; Amad; and Mishal. On the west, the boundary touches Carmel and Shihor-Libnath. Then it turns toward the east to Beth-Dagon. And it touches the territory of Zebulun and the valley of Iphtah-El. Then it goes north of Beth-Emek and Neiel, going out to Cabul, on the left. Then it goes to Abdon; Rehob; Hammon; Kanah; as

far as Sidon the Great. Then the border turns back toward
Ramah, reaching the strong, walled city of Tyre. Then the border
turns toward Hosah. It ends at the Mediterranean Sea. This was
in the areas of Achzib; Ummah; Aphek; and Rehob. There were
22 towns, along with their villages. This is the land-inheritance
of the tribe of the sons of Asher, according to their clans—these
towns, along with their villages.

Naphtali's Share

The sixth prophecy that was assigned by the lot for the tribe of
Naphtali was received, according to their clans. Their boundary
line starts from Heleph at the oak tree in the Zaanannim area,
going through Adami-Nekeb and Jabneel, as far as Lakkum. It
ends at the Jordan River. Then the border turns back to the west
through Aznoth-Tabor. It goes out from there to Hukkok. And it
touches the territory of Zebulun on the south, and the territory
of Asher on the west, and the Jordan River on the east. There
were some strong, walled cities inside these borders: Ziddim;
Zer; Hammath; Rakkath; Chinnereth; Adamah; Ramah; Hazor;
Kedesh; Edrei; En-Hazor; Yiron; Migdal-El; Horem; Beth-Anath;
and Beth-Shemesh. There were 19 towns, along with their villages. This is the land-inheritance of the tribe of the sons of
Naphtali, according to their clans, towns, and villages.

Dan's Share

The seventh prophecy that was assigned by the lot for the tribe of the
sons of Dan was received, according to their clans. Their land-
inheritance included: Zorah; Eshtaol; Ir-Shemesh; Shaalabbin;
Aijalon; Ithlah; Elon; Timnah; Ekron; Eltekeh; Gibbethon;
Baalath; Jehud; Bene-Berak; Gath-Rimmon; Me-Jarkon; and
Rakkon, along with the territory near Joppa. When the territory

of the sons of Dan got away from them, they went up north and fought against Leshem. After they captured it, they put it to the sword and seized it. Then they settled in Leshem, but they named it "Dan," after the name of Dan, their ancestor. This is the land-inheritance of the tribe of the sons of Dan, according to their clans—these towns, along with their villages.

Joshua's Share

When the Israelite leaders finished distributing the various territories of the land-inheritances, the people of Israel gave to Joshua the son of Nun a land-inheritance which was among them. They gave Joshua the town for which he asked, just as the Lord had commanded. The town was Timnath-Serah located in the hill-country of Ephraim. So Joshua built up that town and settled in it.

So these are the land-inheritances which were distributed by lot by Eleazar the high priest, Joshua the son of Nun, and the heads of the fathers' households of the tribes of the people of Israel at Shiloh in the presence of the Lord, at the entrance of the Tabernacle. So they finished dividing all the land of Canaan. *Lord, the first shall be last; Joshua was the last to receive his land-inheritance. Let me be last, for I want to serve You the most.*

The Cities of Refuge

SCRIPTURE: JOSHUA 20

Then the Lord spoke to Joshua: "Tell the Israelites to choose the special
    towns for safe havens (these cities were asylums to which a per-
    son accused of murder could flee, until the heat of passion sub-
    sided. Then a fair trial would be conducted by the impartial
    priests to determine whether the homicide was premeditated or
    unintentional. Because these six cities were spaced out equally, it
    took less than one day's journey to arrive at any one of them to
    receive full protection), just as I told you through Moses.
    Suppose a person accidentally kills someone, not intending to
    kill that individual. If that happens, then that person may go to
    a safe haven city to escape from the man who is looking for
    revenge. When he runs away to one of those special towns, he
    must stop at the entrance gate of the town (where official busi-
    ness was conducted) to explain to the elders of that town what
    happened regarding the accidental death. Then they must permit
    him to enter their town, and give him a place to live among
    them." *Lord, thank You for looking after those who made a mis-
    take. That means You'll take care of me when I make a mistake.*

"However, suppose the avenger who is chasing him follows him to that
    town. If that happens, the elders of the town must not surrender
    the slayer to the pursuer. They must protect him because he
    killed that individual accidentally. It was not out of anger; he did
    not plan ahead of time to kill that individual. The accused man
    should stay in that town until he has been judged by the court
    there. And he should stay inside the safe haven town until the
    current high priest dies. After that time, the slayer may return to

his own home, in the town from which he ran away." *Lord, thank You for man-made laws that protect me.*

So the Israelites set aside some cities to be special towns for safe havens. These towns were: Kedesh in Galilee in the hills of the territory of Naphtali; Shechem among the hills of the territory of Ephraim; and Kiriath-Arba that is, Hebron in the hills of the territory of Judah. On the east side of the Jordan River near Jericho, in the desert in the tableland of the tribe of Reuben, they designated Bezer; Ramoth-in-Gilead among the tribe of Gad; and Golan in Bashan, from the tribe of Manasseh. These were the towns designated for all the people of Israel and for the foreigners who lived among them.

Why these towns? So that if anyone unintentionally killed a person, then he could escape to one of these special towns. This way, no one who killed someone accidentally would die by the hand of the avenger of blood until the person stood trial. *Lord, judge me by what I intend to do, not by those unintentional mistakes I make.*

The Cities of the Levites

SCRIPTURE: JOSHUA 21

The leaders of the fathers of the Levites went near to talk to Eleazar, the
high priest. They also talked to Joshua the son of Nun and to the
leaders of the fathers of all the other tribes of the sons of Israel.
This occurred at the town of Shiloh, in the land of Canaan. The
Levitical leaders said, "Through Moses, the Lord commanded
that you give to us Levites, towns where we may live. And He
commanded that you give pastures to us for our animals." (The
48 towns [see 1 Chron. 6:54-81] to which the Levites were enti-
tled were located within the territory of every tribe of Israel.) So
the Israelites obeyed this commandment of the Lord. The
Israelites gave some towns and pastures to the Levite people out
of their own land-inheritances: the property that was assigned by
lot for the clans of the Kohathites was received. Now those
Levites who were descendants of Aaron, the high priest, received
13 towns from the tribes of Judah, Simeon, and Benjamin by
lot. But the rest of the clans received ten towns by lot. They got
the ten towns from the clans of the tribe of Ephraim, the tribe of
Dan, and the western half-tribe of Manasseh by lot. The Levites
from the Gershonite clans received 13 towns by lot. These
13 towns were located in the territory of the tribe of Issachar,
the tribe of Asher, the tribe of Naphtali, and the eastern half-
tribe of Manasseh in Bashan. The Levites from the Merarite clans
received 12 towns by lot. These 12 towns were located in the
territory of the tribes of Reuben, Gad, and Zebulun.

So the Israelites gave, by lot, to the Levites these 48 towns and their
surrounding pasturelands, just as the Lord had commanded

them through Moses. *Lord, it's wonderful how Your people looked after Your spiritual leaders back then; may we look after them today.*

The following are the names of the towns that were given out of the territory of the tribe of the sons of Judah and out of the tribe of the sons of Simeon. The first set of towns assigned by lot was received for the descendants of Aaron. The Aaronites were one of the clans of the Kohathites who were also from the tribe of Levi. The Israelites gave Kiriath-Arba that is Hebron and all of its surrounding pasturelands to the priests. This city was in the mountains of Judah. But the bigger fields and the villages around the city of Kiriath-Arba had already been given to Caleb the son of Jephunneh for his property. So the Israelites gave the city of Hebron and its pasturelands to the descendants of Aaron, the high priest. (Hebron was also a safe-haven town for those who accidentally killed somebody.) In addition, the Israelites also gave the priests these towns: Libnah and its pastureland; Jattir and its pastureland; Eshtemoa and its pastureland; Holon and its pastureland; Debir and its pastureland; Ain and its pastureland; Juttah and its pastureland; and Beth-Shemesh and its pastureland. There were nine towns given out of the tribe of Judah and the tribe of Simeon.

The Israelites also gave to the Aaronites some towns from the tribe of Benjamin. These towns were: Gibeon and its pastureland; Geba and its pastureland; Anathoth and its pastureland; Almon and its pastureland—four towns for the priests.

So these towns were given to the priests. These priests were from the family of Aaron. The total number of priestly towns and their pasturelands was 13.

The other Kohathite clans of the Levites were given, by lot, these towns out of the territory of the tribe of Ephraim: the city of Shechem and its pastureland in the hills of Ephraim. (Shechem was also a safe-haven town for those who accidentally killed somebody.) The Israelites also gave Gezer and its pastureland; and Kibzaim and its pastureland; and Beth-Horon and its pastureland—four towns for the Levites.

The Israelites also gave to the Levites some towns from the tribe of Dan. These towns were: Elteke and its pastureland; Gibbethon and its pastureland; Aijalon and its pastureland; Gath-Rimmon and its pastureland—four towns for the Levites.

The Israelites gave to the Levites, out of the territory of the western half-tribe of Manasseh: Taanach and its pastureland, and Gath-Rimmon and its pastureland—two towns for the Levites.

So these towns were given to the Levites from the three remaining clans of the Kohathites. The total number of Levite towns and their pasturelands was ten.

The Gershonite clans of the Levite tribe were given these towns: Golan including its pastureland in the Bashan area from the eastern half-tribe of Manasseh. (Golan was also a safe-haven town for those who accidentally killed somebody.) Also, Be-Eshtarah and its pastureland—two towns for the Levites.

The Israelites also gave the Levites from the territory of the tribe of Issachar these towns: Kishion and its pastureland; Daberath and its pastureland; Jarmuth and its pastureland; and En-Gannim and its pastureland—four towns for the Levites.

The Israelites also gave the Levites from the territory of the tribe of Asher these towns: Mishal and its pastureland; Abdon and its pastureland; Helkath and its pastureland; and Rehob and its pastureland—four towns for the Levites.

The Israelites also gave the Levites from the territory of the tribe of Naphtali these towns: Kedesh and its pastureland in Galilee. (Kedesh was a safe-haven town for those who accidentally killed somebody.) Also, Hammoth-Dor and its pastureland; and Kartan and its pastureland—three towns for the Levites.

So the total number received by Gershonite clans was 13 towns and their pasturelands.

The Merarite clans, the remainder of the Levite tribe were given these towns from the territory of the tribe of Zebulun: Jokneam and its pastureland; Kartah and its pastureland; Dimnah and its pastureland; and Nahalal and its pastureland—four towns for the Levites.

The Israelites also gave the Levites from the territory of the tribe of Reuben these towns: Bezer and its pastureland; Jahaz and its pastureland; Kedemoth and its pastureland; and Mephaath and its pastureland—four towns for the Levites.

The Israelites also gave the Levites from the territory of the tribe of Gad these towns: Ramoth-in-Gilead and its pastureland. (Ramoth-in-Gilead was also a safe-haven town for those who accidentally killed somebody.) Also, Mahanaim and its pastureland; Hesbon and its pastureland; and Jazer and its pastureland—a total of four towns for the Levites.

So the total number of towns received, by lot, for the Merarite clans was 12. This was the remainder of the Levite clans.

Therefore, a total of 48 towns and their pasturelands were given to the Levites. All these towns were in the land controlled by the Israelites. Each and every town had a pastureland around it. *Lord, this chapter is a wonderful picture of how Your people took care of those who led them spiritually.*

Israel Settles in the Land

So the Lord gave to Israel all the land of Canaan which He vowed to
give to their ancestors. And after they took possession of it, the
Israelites settled in it. The Lord permitted the Israelites to have
peace on all sides of Canaan, according to what He had sworn
to their ancestors. None of their enemies could withstand them.
The Lord put all of their enemies into their hands. The Lord kept
every promise that He had made to the Israelites. Each one
came true. *Lord, yes Your promises are good and You keep Your
Word.*

The Eastern Tribes Are Sent Home

SCRIPTURE: JOSHUA 22

Then Joshua summoned the tribe of Reuben, the tribe of Gad, and the eastern half-tribe of Manasseh. He said to them, "You have obeyed everything that Moses commanded you. He was the servant of the Lord. You have also obeyed all of my commands. All this time (seven years), you have not abandoned your Hebrew brothers. You have been very careful to obey all the commands of the Lord your God. And now, the Lord your God has given your Hebrew brothers rest, just as He promised to them. So now, turn and go to your homes (Joshua was discharging them to go back to their families who had been left in fortified cities [see Num. 32:17]) in the land where your possession is located. Moses, the servant of the Lord gave that to you on the east side of the Jordan River. However, you must continue to obey the commands and the teachings that Moses, the servant of the Lord ordered you—to love the Lord your God, and to live by His standards; to keep His commands; to cling to Him, and to serve Him with your whole being." *Lord, when we are discharged from our human responsibilities, we still have our responsibility to You. I will love You with all my heart.*

Then Joshua blessed them, and he dismissed them. They went to their homes. Moses had given the area of Bashan to the eastern half-tribe of Manasseh. Along with their Hebrew brothers, Joshua gave more land on the west side of the Jordan River to the western half-tribe of Manasseh. Then Joshua sent them back to their homes, and Joshua also blessed them. *Lord, thank You for man's blessings.*

Joshua said to them: "Go back to your homes and your great possessions. You now have a tremendous number of animals, and lots
of silver, gold, bronze, and iron. And you have many, many
beautiful clothes. You have captured many things of your enemies. You should divide up these things among your Hebrew
brothers." *Lord, I will share.*

So the tribe of Reuben, the tribe of Gad, and the half-tribe of Manasseh
turned and left the other Israelites. They left Shiloh in the land
of Canaan to go back to the land of Gilead, which they owned.
It was their possession just as the Lord had commanded them
through Moses.

The tribe of Reuben, the tribe of Gad, and the eastern half-tribe of
Manasseh traveled to Geliloth near the Jordan River in the land
of Canaan. They built a large, impressive altar there beside the
river (probably on the eastern side of the Jordan River). But the
other Israelites who were still at Shiloh heard about that altar.
They said: "Listen, the tribe of Reuben, the tribe of Gad, and the
half-tribe of Manasseh have built an altar across from the land of
Canaan in Geliloth-Jordan at our border." (The Israelites at
Shiloh suspected that the Trans-Jordanic tribes had apostatized,
having built some sort of idolatrous altar. The clear-cut assump-
tion is that there could be only one authorized altar of Yahweh,
the one true God. And the specific location was at the
Tabernacle.) And when all the Israelites heard that news, the
whole assembly gathered together at Shiloh to go to war against
the tribe of Reuben, the tribe of Gad, and the eastern half-tribe
of Manasseh. *Lord, rumors divide Your people and lead to fights.*

So the Israelites at Shiloh sent a delegation led by Phinehas to the land
of Gilead—to the tribe of Reuben, the tribe of Gad, and to the
eastern half-tribe of Manasseh. Phinehas was the son of Eleazar,
the high priest. Along with Phinehas, they sent ten chiefs—one
chief from each of the tribal families of Israel. Each one of them

was the head of a family of their fathers. They represented the thousands of people in Israel.

So this delegation went to the land of Gilead, to the tribe of Reuben, the tribe of Gad, and the eastern half-tribe of Manasseh, and spoke to them: "The entire community of the Lord is asking you: 'Why are you sinning against the God of Israel by turning away from Him today? Why did you build that rival altar for yourselves? (Implying they were seceding from their Hebrew brothers.) You know that such a thing is against God's law. Remember what happened at Peor? We still suffer today because of that sin. A plague came upon the entire community of the Lord (see Num. 25:1-9). And now you are doing the same thing. Aren't you turning against the Lord? Will you refuse to follow the Lord? If you don't stop your rebellions today, the Lord will become angry with everyone in Israel tomorrow. If the land you own is truly unclean, then cross over into the Lord's land where His Holy Tabernacle dwells. Take for yourselves some property among us. But whatever you do, don't rebel against the Lord or against us, causing us to look like rebels. How? By building yourselves an unauthorized altar, in addition to the true altar of the Lord our God. Remember what happened to Achan, the son of Zerah? He truly refused to obey the command about what must be completely destroyed. That one man broke God's law, but all Israel was punished. Achan died because of his own sin, but many other people died, too.'" *Lord, may I seek out the truth, and not listen to rumors.*

The tribe of Reuben, the tribe of Gad, and the eastern half-tribe of Manasseh answered the representative heads saying: "The Lord is the one true God. Again we say, the Lord is the one true God. He knows why we did this. And concerning Israel, He would know if it were in rebellion, and if it were a betrayal against Him. You can understand it, too. If you believe that we have done something wrong, you may kill us. If we did turn away from following the Lord by building for ourselves an unauthorized altar, then may the Lord Himself punish us. If we built that altar to offer whole burnt offerings, or for food offerings, or for putting peace offering sacrifices on it, then may the Lord Himself punish us." *Lord, it seems as if people have always argued over the practice of religion.*

"No! We did not build that altar for those reasons. We were afraid that, some day in the future, your sons may say to our sons: 'You cannot worship the Lord, the God of Israel.' The Lord has put a barrier between us and you—you sons of Reuben and you sons of Gad—it's the Jordan River. You have no share in the Lord. So we were afraid that your sons might force our sons to stop worshiping the Lord. So we said to ourselves, "Let's start building an altar for ourselves—not for the whole burnt offerings or for sacrificing—but to be a witness between us and you, and between our generations after us, so that we worship the Lord in His presence (at the Tabernacle) with our whole burnt offerings and sacrifices and peace offerings. We didn't want your sons to say to our sons at some future day: 'You people of Gilead have no share in the Lord.'" *Lord, it's good to solve problems before they become problems.*

"We thought: 'If, in the future, your sons say such a thing to us or to our descendants, we would say: "Look at the altar of the Lord which our forefathers made, not for whole burnt offerings or for sacrificing, but to be a witness between us and you."' Far be it from us to rebel against the Lord or to turn away from following the Lord today by building an altar for whole burnt offerings, for food offerings, and for sacrificing separately from the true altar of the Lord, our God, which is in front of the Tabernacle." *Lord, I will worship You in the right way at the right place.*

Phinehas the priest and the ten chiefs of the assembly heard this explanation of the tribe of Reuben, and the tribe of Gad, and the half-tribe of Manasseh. The representatives of the thousands of people in Israel who were with Phinehas heard it too. So the delegation was pleased. So Phinehas, the son of Eleazar the high priest, spoke to the Reubenites, the Gadites, and the Manassites saying, "Today we know that the Lord is with us, because you surely did not turn against the Lord as we had thought. We are happy that any Israelites will not be punished by the Lord for this deed." *Lord, thank You for level-headed spiritual leaders.*

Then Phinehas, the son of Eleazar the high priest, and the ten chiefs, returned to the land of Canaan from the Reubenites and the Gadites out of the land of Gilead. The delegation came back to the people of Israel, reporting to them what had happened. The Israelites were also pleased and happy, so that they praised God. And they decided not to go to war against the tribes of Reuben and Gad and not to destroy the lands where they lived (civil war was narrowly averted). And the tribe of Reuben and the tribe of Gad proclaimed regarding that altar at Geliloth-Jordan: "It is a witness between us that the Lord is the one true God." *Lord, it's good to live peaceably with the brethren.*

Joshua Speaks to the Leaders of Israel

SCRIPTURE: JOSHUA 23

The Lord gave Israel rest from all their enemies that surrounded them. After time went by (perhaps 20 years), Joshua was old. So he summoned all Israel (to the Tabernacle at Shiloh)—their elders and their leaders, their judges and their officers. He said to them, "I am now very old. You have seen everything that the Lord your God has done to all of these nations for your sake. It was the Lord your God who was fighting for you. Listen, I have assigned to you land-inheritances for your tribes from those nations that remain. In addition, I have assigned all the other nations that I have already conquered—from the Jordan River to the Mediterranean Sea in the west. The Lord your God will expel them ahead of you. He will force them out as you advance. And you will seize their land, just as the Lord your God promised to you." *Lord, I claim Your promises as my own.*

"Be very strong. You must be very careful to obey everything that is written in the Book of the Law, consisting of Genesis, Exodus, Leviticus, Numbers, and Deuteronomy, of Moses. Don't turn away from it, either to the right or to the left. You must not associate with these nations that are still remaining among your people. Don't even mention the names of their gods or take an oath by those gods. Don't serve them or bow yourselves down to them. No, you must continue to cling to the Lord your God, just as you have done until today. The Lord has forced out great and strong nations ahead of you. As for you, none have been able to withstand you so far. One Israelite could defeat 1,000 enemies, because it is the Lord your God who is fighting for you, just as

He promised to you. So you must really watch yourselves: keep loving the Lord your God." *Lord, I will separate.*

"However, if you defect from God and join what's left of these nations which remain among your people, intermarrying with them, and you associate with them, and they associate with you, then, you can be sure that the Lord your God will not continue to force out these nations ahead of you. Instead, they will become a snare and a trap for you. They will be like a whip on your back and thorns in your eyes, until you disappear from this good land which the Lord your God has given to you." *Lord, I will get rid of sin in my life.*

"Now listen, I'm about to die. You know with all your heart and soul, that every single good thing that the Lord your God promised concerning you has come true. Not one promise has failed. Every good thing that the Lord your God said has come true for you. And in the same way, the Lord will bring all kinds of terrible things upon you, until the Lord your God destroys you from off this good land that He has given to you. If you break the covenant of the Lord your God which He commanded you to obey, and if you go and serve different gods and bow down to them, then the Lord's anger will burn against you. And you will soon perish from off the good land that He has given to you." *Lord, I cannot leave You, I fear the results.*

Joshua's Farewell Speech at Shechem

SCRIPTURE: JOSHUA 24

Joshua gathered together all the tribes of Israel to Shechem, summoning the elders, the top leaders, the judges, and the officials of Israel. They all presented themselves to the presence of the one true God. *Lord, it's good to gather in Your presence.*

Then Joshua said to all the people, "This is what the Lord, the God of Israel says: 'In the past, your ancestors lived beyond the Euphrates River. They worshiped different gods. Terah was the father of Nahor and Abraham. I took Abraham, your ancestor, from beyond the Euphrates River, and I caused him to travel throughout all the land of Canaan. I multiplied his descendants. I gave Isaac to him. And I gave Jacob and Esau to Isaac. I gave the Mount Seir region to Esau to possess, while Jacob and his sons went down to Egypt. I sent Moses and Aaron, and then I brought plagues upon Egypt. Later, I brought you out, bringing your parents out of Egypt. You went into the Red Sea, and the Egyptians chased after your parents with chariots and horsemen into the Red Sea. The people cried out to Me for help, and I put thick darkness between you and the Egyptians. I caused the sea to drown the Egyptians. Your eyes have seen what I have done in Egypt. Then you lived in the desert for many years. Next, I brought you into the land of the Amorites who were living east of the Jordan River. They battled you, but I gave you victory over them. As you advanced, I destroyed them. You seized their land. Balak (the son of Zippor, the king of Moab) rose up and fought against Israel. He sent some messengers to Balaam (the son of Beor) and hired him to put a curse on you. However, I did not listen to Balaam. Instead, Balaam blessed you again and again. I rescued you from his power."' *Lord, it's good to receive Your past blessings in my life.*

"'Then you crossed the Jordan River and came to Jericho. The masters of Jericho fought against you. So did the Amorites, the Perizzites, the Canaanites, the Hittites, the Girgashites, the Hivites, and the Jebusites. But I gave you victory over them all. I sent the hornet (see Deut. 7:20) ahead of you. You destroyed those two Amorites kings as you advanced. It was not by your sword or by your bow. I have given you a land for which you did not work. I have given you towns which you did not build. That is where you live now. You are eating fruit, but you did not plant the vineyards or the olive trees.'" *Lord, it's not I but Christ.*

"So now you people need to revere the Lord and serve Him with sincerity and truth. Turn away from the gods which your ancestors served beyond the Euphrates River and in Egypt. Serve the Lord. But if it seems wrong to you to serve the Lord, then you must make a choice today as to whom you will serve—either the gods whom your ancestors who lived beyond the Euphrates River, or the gods of the Amorites who used to live where you now live. However, as for me and my family, we will serve YAHWEH." *Lord, I join with Joshua—I will serve You.*

Then the people of Israel answered, "We will never abandon the Lord to serve other gods, because the Lord is our God. He is the One who brought us and our parents out of the land of Egypt, out of that house of slavery. Before our very eyes, He performed those great miracles. He has guarded us wherever we have gone, and among all the ethnic groups with whom we have come in contact. The Lord has forced out all the ethnic groups that faced us, especially the Amorites who lived in the land. Yes, we will serve the Lord because He is our God." *Lord, thank You for past victories.*

Then Joshua said to the people, "You must serve the Lord, because He is
a holy God. He is a jealous God. He will not forgive your rebellions or your sins if you abandon the Lord and serve unauthorized gods. No, He will turn away from you and do harm to
you. He will eat you up...after all the good He has done for
you."

But the people said to Joshua, "No, we will serve the Lord." *Lord, that's
my passion.*

Then Joshua said to the people, "You are witnesses against yourselves
that you have chosen the Lord for yourselves—to serve Him."

And they said, "Yes, that's what we are testifying." *Lord, I surrender all
to You.*

Joshua said, "Then you must now turn away from unauthorized gods
which are still among you. Give your hearts over to the Lord,
the God of Israel." *Lord, show me anything in my life that hin-
ders my worship of You.*

The people said to Joshua, "We will serve our God, the Lord. We will
obey Him." *Lord, me too.*

That day, Joshua made a covenant with the people of Israel. (This was
not a new covenant but a *renewal* of the same covenant which
had been made with the people of Israel at Mount Sinai. See
Deuteronomy 29:1-29.) At Shechem, Joshua wrote for them
decrees and laws. And, Joshua recorded these words in the Book
of the Law of God. Then he took a large stone and set it up
under the oak tree that was next to the altar of the Lord. (This
was the spot where Abraham and Jacob had offered sacrifices
and worshiped God [see Gen. 12:6-8; 35:4].) Then Joshua said
to all the people, "Listen, this stone is a witness against us. It has
heard all the sayings of the Lord that He spoke to us. It will give

testimony against you if you tell a lie against your God." *Lord, I write down my commitment to You.*

Then Joshua sent the people away. Each one went to the land-inheritance which God had given to him.

The Death of Joshua and Eleazar

Sometime later, Joshua, the son of Nun, the servant of the Lord, died. He was 110 years old. They buried him within the borders of his inheritance in Timnath-Serah, which is in the hills of Ephraim, north of the hill of Gaash. And the people of Israel served the Lord while Joshua was still alive, and as long as the elders were alive. Some of them outlived Joshua. They knew (experientially) every deed that the Lord had done for Israel. *Lord, I too will die; may I be faithful to death, as was Joshua.*

At Shechem, the people also buried the bones of Joseph which the Israelites had brought up from Egypt (see Gen. 50:22-26). They did this in the part of the field that Jacob had purchased for 100 pieces of silver from the son of Hamor (see Gen. 33:18-19; 47:28-30). He was the father of Shechem. This is what the descendants of Joseph inherited. Later, Eleazar (a nephew of Moses) the son of Aaron, died. And they buried him at Gibeah, the town that belonged to Phinehas, his son. Phinehas received this village among the hills of the half-tribe of Ephraim. *Lord, You bury Your servants but Your work goes on.*

The Choice Offered by Joshua

Joshua gathered all the tribes...and they presented themselves before God. "I have given you a land for which you did not labor, and cities which you did not build, and you dwell in them; you eat of the vineyards and olive groves which you did not plant...'put away the gods which your father served...choose for yourselves this day whom you will serve...But as for me and my house, we will serve the Lord'" (Joshua 24:1,13-15).

Joshua gave one of the greatest "choice" speeches ever. Why is this called one of the greatest "decision" speeches? Because Joshua was calling people to choose God, the greatest choice ever. Because Joshua was calling for a decision he had personally made. Because Joshua was calling a new generation to spiritual commitment. Because as Joshua was facing death, he wanted to extend his spiritual influences beyond his physical life.

The nation of Israel had captured the Promised Land and subdued the occupants. They have fought 31 major battles. Some battles were in the open field. Some battles captured major fortified cities. Some battles were against cavalry and armed chariots. But God was with them and they won all the battles. (Even though they were at first defeated at Ai, eventually they won.) *Lord, thank You for the victories in my life.*

Israel should have been more spiritual than ever because God had been with them in battle. They should have been more grateful to God because He had given everything this former slave nation needed—land, houses, fruit trees, walls, cities, etc. But after their victory, their faith became lukewarm, their commitment became lax. They should have worshiped more than ever, but they became busy with the things God had given them. They quickly forgot about God. *Lord, I will always remember You.*

Like some who often win a war, but lose the peace, Israel didn't know how to live victorious for God after they won battles for God. They were like some Christians who must have a weekly battle to keep serving Christ. They must continually fight or march to demonstrate their commitment to Christ. Is that your problem? Are you one who used to serve God faithfully when you needed God to solve your problems? But now that things are easy, your commitment to Christ has taken a back seat? Do you need to be called back to complete commitment? Do you need to make a decision to serve God, but just can't do it? If so, today you need to examine the decision-making process, so you will know how to get your spiritual fervor back. *Lord, keep me close to You.*

Do you make decisions—both big and small—without any thought of strategy? When you learn how to properly make decisions, you take control of your life. Correct decisions can guide your life to become what you dreamed it to be. Those who don't know what they want to do usually end up doing many things they don't want to do. If you don't control your daily decisions, you will eventually go where you don't want to go.

Joshua was challenging the older people who entered the Promised Land with him. They had dreamed with him, fought with him. They all had relatives who died fighting under Joshua in various battles. But now Joshua challenges them to holiness. "Put away the gods which your fathers served" (Josh. 24:14). *Lord, I will be clean.*

Notice some of the factors in good decision making. We sometimes need biblical leaders to motivate us to make correct decisions. Joshua called all Israel together, then told them what they should do. How has your pastor and others influenced your thinking? When they point you to the Bible, do you obey what the Scriptures command? *Lord, thank You for counselors.*

When you enter God's presence, you get divine guidance in making choices. "They presented themselves before God" (Josh. 24:1). This involves fellowshipping with God, asking for direction, and listening for His voice. It's easy to make the decisions God wants you to make when you feel His presence about you. *Lord, I feel Your presence.*

Did you see the examples that Joshua held before them? Examples of Abraham, Isaac, Jacob, and Moses (see Josh. 24:2,4,5). To become good, you must look to good heroes; and to become victorious, make *overcomers* your heroes. Then Joshua held before them decisive events that brought them into the land. Joshua reminded them how God defeated the Egyptians, the Amorites, and Jericho (Josh 24: 6-8,11). Since God had given victory to their fathers, He could do it for them. We all have heroes and our heroes influence us. What heroes motivate you? Study them to see how they made proper decisions. *Lord, I choose those heroes who have chosen to follow You.*

Next, Joshua appealed to gratitude. He reminded the people of God's blessing in their lives. They farmed land that God gave them. They lived in houses they didn't build, and they picked fruit from trees they didn't plant. God had given the land to them. Now in gratitude, God wanted their obedience and worship. Of all the virtues, gratitude is the least remembered by people of little character. Why, because gratitude always thinks of the other person. Gratitude seeks nothing in return. Being grateful for good things is the God-thing to do. It is kindness personified. *Lord, I am grateful for what You have done for me.*

What did Joshua want them to do? He wanted everyone to fear God, serve Him sincerely and in truth. Sincerely meant with all their hearts—from the bottom of their hearts. He wanted a total emotional response of love. He didn't want half-hearted love, Joshua called for total commitment. Are you there? Do you love God will all your being? That doesn't mean being a religious fanatic, nor does it mean to respond with an emotional eruption. It means you should love God totally, in your own quiet way if you are a quiet person. It means loving God loudly and expressively if you are an exuberant person. *Lord, I love You inwardly with all my heart. Help me express it outwardly the way You express Yourself.*

But Joshua also wanted people to love God "in truth." That means loving God the way the Bible tells you to do it, not the way your friends do it, nor the way that feels good to you. To love God "in truth" is to love God according to the truth. Remember, Jesus said He was the truth (John 14:6). *Lord, teach me the truth.*

The speech got results. The people said, "The Lord our God we will serve, and His voice we will obey" (Josh. 24:24). When people make a decision—a great one—there should be an outward sign. Today we sign a contract or shake hands, and in church we go to the altar or make our commitment public. How did Joshua make their commitment public? "Joshua wrote these words in the Book of the Law of God. "And he took a large stone, and set it up there under the oak that was by the sanctuary of the Lord" (Josh. 24:26). Do you see how the people's decision ends? At the Sanctuary of God! They made their vow in the presence of God—where God lives—and chiseled their commitment on a monument. Like the statues and commemorative stones in our city parks, Joshua wrote the words of their decisions in stone to remind them and future generations what they decided. *Lord, I will write my decisions in my heart, which is better than chiseling them in stone.*

Are you in the presence of God as you read these words? Is your life a sanctuary? Have you decided to give the Lord everything? Make that decision; write it in your Bible and sign it. Then do something symbolic to tell the world that, "I have decided to follow Jesus, no turning back." *Lord, I will.*

My Time to Pray

Lord, I have decided to follow You wholly;
    I will not turn back.

Lord, I will gaze into Your face totally;
    I will not look back.

Lord, I will worship You with my whole heart;
    I will not draw back.

       Amen.

PRAYING JUDGES
TO SEE LIGHT IN A TIME OF DARKNESS

INTRODUCTION

The old man wrote at a crude table under the fig tree in the backyard of his home in Shiloh. Under the shade of a fig tree was where a man went to pray, or to meditate, or be with God. That's why Samuel retreated there often, he wanted to be with God; but more importantly, he wanted God to be with him. *Lord, give me that passion.*

Samuel had been dedicated to God since birth, his mother Hannah had asked God for a son, so when he was born; she named him Samuel—his name means "to ask." *Lord, give me faith to ask things of You.*

Samuel knew he was living on the cusp of a new era in God's plans. He saw God's earthly kingdom coming. He would anoint Saul to be the first king of Israel and then he would anoint David.

Samuel knew the kingdom would be glorious under David, because David was a man after God's own heart. Israel would have protection and peace under David that they didn't have under the judges. There would be a strong central government, not sectional bickering and the civil war of the judges. There would be a strong spiritual unity around the Tabernacle. There would no longer be apostate priests and people building shrines to idols in their homes as they did during the judges. *Lord, thank You for a government of laws.*

Samuel determined to link the coming priestly kingdom of David to the past victories of Joshua who conquered the Promised Land. Between these two bright periods of time, there was a period of 300 years called the "Dark Ages" of Jewish history. Samuel thought, "If I wrote how truly bad the time of the judges was, then maybe future generations will learn from their failure." *Lord, I will learn. I will not repeat their errors.*

Samuel would write in the Book of Judges that Israel was not united, but each family tribe was just that, a tribe that was not ruled by laws. Isn't the rule of law the first step of civilization? And these judges were just tribesmen leaders. They were the spiritual ancestors of what the godly kingdom was to become. Each judge was a patriot who sacrificed everything to rally their fellow tribesmen to fight off attacks. Each judge brought in a time of security and prosperity. Each judge was a ruthless religious reformer such as Luther, Calvin, and Wesley. Through reforming the people spiritually, they reformed society and gave a better life to their followers. Their embryonic tribal rule prepared Israel for the coming rule by national kings. *Lord, thank You for judges.*

The word *judge* means one who sits at a bar to decide cases based on the law. Each judge did that, as Deborah made decisions under a palm tree. But each also picked up the sword to defend the law. Also, they stood before their tribes to teach the law. To each judge, national security and spiritual prosperity were inseparable. *Lord, I pray for revival and peace in my nation, for those two are still inseparable.*

Samuel thought back over the past 300 years. Those were good days, yet those were hard days...demanding days...exasperating days. Samuel smiled, "Every man did right in his own eyes." He would write that key phrase several times in the Book, because, "In those days there was no king" (Judg. 21:25). *Lord, our problem will not be gone till Jesus the King rules.*

Two feats stood out in Samuel's mind. First was the utter failure of the people to govern themselves and remain faithful to God. Second, the continual mercy of God, that when the people cried out to God, He sent them a judge to deliver them. *Lord, thank You for mercy.*

Samuel would tell of 12 judges raised up by God to deliver His people from disunion and dissension. (We don't know much about some of the judges.) The number 12 reminded Samuel of the 12 sons of Jacob. God liked that number, but God also likes the number seven. Samuel would emphasize...seven cycles...seven victories...and seven judges. Each cycle would follow the same sequence. There would be seven apostasies, seven oppressions by an enemy, seven times of spiritual repentance, and seven judges who would deliver. *Lord, thank You for Your faithfulness when Your people are not faithful.*

In Judges there was no unifying king and there was no Israel-wide victory and peace. The Book of Judges is about the tension of tribal disunity against partial unity. Read the stories carefully. There was not one common enemy against all Israel. The Philistines attacked from the south, the Canaanites attacked from the north. Moab and Ammon attacked from across the Jordan to the east. Then from the extreme southern desert, the Midianites attacked; partial attacks, partial victories, and partial peace. Some tribes were in servitude to an oppressor when other tribes had just defeated their oppressor and were enjoying peace. *Lord, I want total victory in my life, but when I get victory in one area; I struggle in another. My life is no different from the period of the judges.*

Samuel would describe these judges accurately, without hiding their weaknesses or sins. He would tell of their exploits and how the Spirit of God came upon them. But these saints had warts and foibles. Samson was a womanizer, Othniel was henpecked, and Gideon was the youngest son from the least family. Then too, Jephthah was the son of a harlot, a Canaanite prostitute at that. *Lord, You used weak and unlikely people in the past. Do it again, use me.*

The Book of Judges is about weaknesses. Weak tribes...weak commitment...weak people, but God helped them though they were unlikely leaders. The spiritual priority is still true, "Not many wise according to the flesh, not many mighty, not many noble, are called" (1 Cor. 1:26). Victory always comes from the Lord when we accept what Christ offered, "My strength is made perfect in weakness" (2 Cor. 12:9).

This is the 39th Bible book I've written and translated in the series, *Praying the Scriptures*. If God speaks to you through this book, then get other books until you pray all the way through the Bible. That's my goal, I plan to translate 27 more Bible books in this series, and then I will have prayed my way through all the 66 books of the Bible.

More Territory Captured

SCRIPTURE: JUDGES 1

Joshua died. Then the people of Israel prayed to the Lord, saying, "Who will be first to go up to fight for us against the Canaanite people?" The Lord said to them, "The tribe of Judah will go up; I have delivered the land into his hand." So the men of Judah said to the men of Simeon, their brothers, (Judah and Simeon shared the same land—inheritance [see Josh. 19:1].) "Come up with us to our allotted land-inheritance. Let us fight together against the Canaanites for our portion. Then we will also go with you to fight for your allotted land-inheritance." Therefore, the Simeonites joined with the men of Judah. So Judah and Simeon went up together into battle. The Lord gave them victory over the Canaanites and the Perizzites. The men of Judah and Simeon defeated 10,000 men at the city of Bezek. There they found Adoni-Bezek, the ruler of the city, and fought against him; and they defeated the Canaanites and the Perizzites. But Adoni-Bezek ran away, so they chased him and caught him. Then they cut off his thumbs and big toes. Then Adoni-Bezek said, "I have cut off the thumbs and big toes of 70 kings. Those kings were gathering scraps of food underneath my table. Now God has paid me back for what I did to them." The men of Judah and Simeon took Adoni-Bezek to Jerusalem, and he died there. *Lord, it's good to have friends to face my spiritual battles with me.*

They fought against Jerusalem and captured it. (Only a part of Jerusalem was taken by the Israelites; they did not conquer the fortress. The Jebusites held out until the time of David [see 2 Sam. 5:6-9].) They used their swords to kill the people, setting the city on fire. Later on, the men of Judah and Simeon went down to fight against more of the Canaanites who lived in the hill-country and in the south, as well as the foothills.

Then the men of Judah and Simeon went to fight against those Canaanites who lived in the city of Hebron. Now the name of Hebron was previously "Kiriath-Arba." They defeated the descendants of Sheshai, Ahiman, and Talmai. Then the men of Judah and Simeon went from Hebron against those who lived in the city of Debir. (And the name of Debir was previously "Kiriath-Sepher.") *Lord, just as Israel had to both defeat an enemy and take possession of the land, so I must get victory over bad habits and establish good habits.*

Caleb said, "I will give Achsah, my daughter, as a wife to the one who attacks Kiriath-Sepher and captures it. Caleb had a younger brother named Kenaz. And, Kenaz had a son named Othniel who captured Kiriath-Sepher. So Caleb gave his daughter Achsah to Othniel to be his wife. When Achsah came to Othniel, she persuaded him to ask her father for some land (as a wedding gift). She got down from her donkey (showing respect for Caleb). Caleb said, "What do you want?" Achsah answered Caleb, "Give me a blessing. You have given me dry land in the Negev (desert). Please give me some land with springs of water." So, Caleb gave her the upper and lower springs. *Lord, teach me to ask in prayer for what I need.*

The Kenite people left Jericho, the City of Palm Trees, and went up with the men of Judah and Simeon. The Kenites went to the desert of Judah to settle with the people there, near the city of Arad. The Kenites were from the family of Moses' father-in-law. Some Canaanite people lived in the city of Zephath. (It was "devoted" to a pagan god.) So the men of Judah and Simeon, their Hebrew brothers, defeated those Canaanites. They completely destroyed the city, and named the city "Hormah." The men of

Judah and Simeon captured Gaza with its territory, Ashkelon with its territory, and Ekron with its territory. The Lord was on the side of the men of Judah and Simeon. They drove out the inhabitants of the hill-country. But they could not force out the people living on the plain. Why? Because those people had iron chariots (iron wheels). *Lord, some habits are hard to give up because they have "iron wheels."*

As Moses had promised, Hebron was given to Caleb. Caleb forced out the three sons of Anak. However, the people of Benjamin could not force the Jebusite people to leave Jerusalem. Since that time, the Jebusites have lived with the Benjaminites in Jerusalem. Also, the men of Joseph went up to fight against the city of Bethel. The Lord was on their side. The men of Joseph scouted the area around Bethel. (Now, the name of that city was previously "Luz" [see Gen. 28:19].) The spies saw a man coming out of the city, and said to him, "Please show us a way into the city. If you help us, then we will protect you." The man showed the spies the secret way into the city. The men of Joseph killed the people in Bethel, but they permitted the man who helped them—including his whole family—to leave. That man went to the land of the Hittite people, and built a city, named "Luz." That is its name today.

Some Land Is Not Taken

There were Canaanites living in Beth-Shan and its villages, in Taanach and its villages, in Dor and its villages, in Ibleam and its villages, and in Megiddo and its villages. The people of Manasseh did not force those people who lived there out of their towns. The Canaanites were determined to stay there. Later, the people of Israel became stronger. They forced the Canaanites to work as slaves for them. However, the Israelites did not completely force

all the Canaanites out of their land. (As God had clearly speci-
fied in Exod. 23:23-24, the Israelites were to exterminate all the
Canaanites, not merely to subjugate them.) There were
Canaanites living in Gezer, but the people of Ephraim did not
force all of those Canaanites out of their land. So the Canaanite
people continued to live in Gezer among the people of Ephraim.
Some Canaanites lived in the cities of Kitron and Nahalol. The
people of Zebulun did not force them out of their land, either.
They stayed among the people of Zebulun. But the Zebulunites
forced them to work as slaves. Neither did the people of Asher
force the Canaanite residents out of the cities of Acco, Sidon,
Ahlab, Achzib, Helbah, Aphik, and Rehob. The people of Asher
did not force the Canaanites out of their land. So the Canaanites
continued to live among the Asherites. The people of Nephtali
did not force the Canaanites out of the cities of Beth-Shemesh
and Beth-Anath. So the people of Naphtali continued to live
among the Canaanites in Beth-Shemesh and Beth-Anath in the
land. Those Canaanite people worked as slaves for the people of
Nephtali. The Amorites confined the Danites to the hill-country.
The Amorites would not permit the Danites to come down to
live in the plain. The Amorites were determined to stay on
Mount Heres, in Aijalon, and in Shaalbim. But the Israelites got
the upper hand. Then the Israelites forced the Amorites to work
as slaves for them. The territory of the Amorites extended from
the Ascent of Akrabbim to Sela and beyond it. *Lord, when Israel
didn't win a complete victory, they later became slaves to those
they didn't vanquish. In the same way, when I don't get victory
over a sin, it becomes my master. I want complete victory.*

Weeping at Bochim

Scripture: Judges 2

The Angel of the Lord went up from Gilgal to Bochim and spoke to the
people of Israel there: "I brought you up from Egypt. I led you
to the land that I promised to give to your forefathers. I said: 'I
will never break My covenant with you. In return, you must not
make a covenant with the people who live in this land. Instead,
you must destroy their altars.' Nevertheless, you did not obey
Me. How could you do such a thing as this? So now, I will not
force the people out of this land who are in your path. No, they
will be like thorns in your sides. Their gods will become a snare
for you." After the Angel of the Lord spoke this message to all
the Israelites, the people cried loudly. So they named that place
"Bochim" (meaning "weepers"). And there they offered sacrifices
to the Lord. (The Israelites were forbidden to offer sacrifices any-
where else except at the Tabernacle, so it must have been here.)
*Lord, I know You are not pleased when I allow sin to reside in my
life.*

Joshua's Death

Then Joshua dismissed the people. So each of the Israelites went to take
possession of his own share of the land. The people of Israel
served the Lord as long as Joshua was alive, and during the life-
times of the elders who lived on after Joshua's time. These people had seen all the awesome things that the Lord had done for
Israel. (Joshua led them for 30 more years [see Josh. 24:29-30].)
Joshua, the son of Nun, the servant of the Lord died at the age

of 110. So the Israelites buried him within the borders of his land-inheritance at Timnath-Heres, in the hill-country of Ephraim, north of Mount Gaash. After the generation that outlived Joshua died, their children grew up, but they did not know the Lord or the awesome deeds that He had done for Israel. *Lord, I will teach those who come after me all the great things You have done for me. May those who come after me do all the things I've done for You: but may they do better things in a better way.*

The Israelites Abandon Yahweh

So the Israelites did what was evil in the sight of the Lord and worshiped Baalim. (Plural, to include all the different gods of Canaan.) The Lord had brought the people of Israel out of the land of Egypt, and their ancestors had worshiped the Lord. But later, the Israelites abandoned the Lord, the God of their forefathers. They began to worship different gods—the gods of the people who lived around them. These Israelites bowed themselves down to those gods. And that made the Lord very angry. These Israelites abandoned the Lord and served Baal and the Ashtareths (female gods). *Lord, I want to please You; I will not worship any other god.*

Yes, the Lord was very angry with the people of Israel. So He allowed plunderers to attack them and take away their possessions. He sold them into the control of their enemies who surrounded them. Israel could not protect themselves from their enemies anymore. Every time the Israelites went out to fight, they lost. Why? Because the Lord was not on their side, just as He had said. The Lord had vowed that this would happen. *Lord, don't leave me.*

Nevertheless, the Lord raised up some judges who rescued the people of Israel from the control of those raiders. Before that the Israelites paid no attention to their judges. Instead, the Israelites were not faithful to God; they followed different gods and bowed themselves down to those false gods. The Israelites stopped obeying the commands of the Lord. They groaned under those who oppressed and afflicted them. Every time the Lord felt sorry for them, He raised up a judge to save them from the control of their enemies. The Lord was with that particular judge. But when each judge died, the Israelites would return to their old sinful ways and behave worse than their ancestors, following after different gods. They would serve them and bow themselves down to them. The Israelites were very stubborn, refusing to change their evil ways. So the Lord became furious with the Israelites, thinking: "This nation has broken My covenant which I made with their ancestors. They have not listened to Me, so I will no longer force out any of the nations who remain in the land since Joshua died. Why? So that I may use those pagan people to test Israel. I will see whether or not Israel will live by My commands as their ancestors did." In the past, the Lord permitted those nations to remain in the land. He did not force them out quickly, not handing them over to Joshua. *Lord, there are many trials and temptations in my life, help me overcome them all. Help me draw near to You.*

Judges 2

The Story Behind Israel Being Persecuted:

The Day the People Cried ⌒ Date: 1425 B.C.

Then the Angel of the Lord...said: "I led you up from Egypt and brought you to the land...But you have not obeyed My voice...I will not drive them out before you; there shall be thorns in your side,

and their gods shall be a snare to you." So it was...that the people
lifted up their voices and wept. Then they called the name of that
place Bochim (weepers) (Judges 2:1-5).

What happens when you only do half of what the Lord commands? What happens when you compromise? Israel had occupied the Promised Land, but they didn't drive out the heathen. They didn't get rid of the false gods in the land. Within time, Israel picked up the sinful habits of the heathen among them, and they began worshiping false gods—probably along with their worship of Jehovah. Are you like Israel, are you becoming more like the unsaved around you? Are you "playing" with the false gods of this age? If so, learn what will happen to you, from what happened to Israel.

First, notice many tribes didn't completely drive out the heathen (see Judg. 1:21,27,29-31,33). What was God's response? When the people stopped fighting, God said, "I will not drive them out from before you" (Judg. 2:3). If you don't try to have victory in your personal life, God will not give it to you. *Lord, I will strive against sin.*

When the people compromised, God did not do miracles for them. Do you see who stopped fighting first, the people or God? There's a lesson for you, God will not work for you if you stop working for Him. *Lord, I will not give up.*

When God told the people that hard times were coming, they wept. You would too. Who likes trouble or problems? God promised the heathen would be thorns in their side, and their gods would entrap them. The people wept so hard and so long that the place was called *Bochim*—weeping. Can you hear a Jewish father tell his son, "Bochim is the place we got the bad news and everyone wept"? *Lord, prepare me for bad news in my life for it's surely coming.*

What should they have done? They should have done what you should do when you get bad news from God. You should do more than weep; you should repent, change your ways, go back to doing what God originally told you to do. Israel should have immediately gone back to war to drive out the enemy from among them. Israel should have gotten rid of their false gods. But they didn't. For the rest of the Book of Judges, Israel was enslaved and persecuted by their enemies and tempted by their gods. All of the misery that Israel suffered in the Book of Judges was the result of their incomplete obedience. *Lord, don't let me compromise.*

Tears are not enough when you've disobeyed God, but tears are a good start. Paul described the Corinthians, "For godly sorrow produces repentance leading to salvation, not to be regretted; but the sorrow of the world produces death" (2 Cor. 7:10). Israel wept in Bochim and as a result, the nation lived godly for one generation. "So the people served the Lord all the days of Joshua, and all the days of the elders who outlived Joshua" (Judg. 2:7). *Lord, I want to be godly.*

There is a cycle in the Book of Judges, and each of the seven main judges was used of God to deliver God's people from their servitude to heathen nations. "The Lord raised up judges who delivered them" (Judg. 2:16). But something happened each time God delivered Israel. "And when the judge was dead, the tribe went back to sin and behaved more corruptly than their fathers, by following other gods, to serving them and bowing down to them. They did not cease from their own doings nor from their stubborn way" (Judg. 2:19). Each time Israel was delivered, the nation eventually fell back into sin. What happened? "And the anger of the Lord was hot against Israel. So He delivered them into the hands of plunderers who despoiled them; and He sold them into the hands of their enemies" (Judg. 2:14). Do you see the cycle? First, Israel sinned; and then second, God allowed an enemy nation to conquer them and persecute them. Third, Israel repented and cried to God for deliverance. Finally in step four, God raised up a deliverer—a judge—to lead them in battle to victory. *Lord, thank You for godly spiritual leaders.*

Where are you in the cycle? Are you on the downward compromising station? Or have you come to the place where you are begging God to deliver you? Are you heading for defeat or coming out of defeat? Is God helping you win a battle over your enemies? Wherever you are, look again at the cycle. This time don't look for yourself in the cycle. Rather look for God. Where is the Lord? He's in every stage of the cycle. When you sin, God is there. He's not there to help you, but to convict you and sometimes to punish you. When Israel "forsook the Lord God of their fathers" (Judg. 2:12), notice what God did: "The hand of the Lord was against them" (Judg. 2:15). God did not help them win their battles. Have you been fighting your own battles lately? Have you been struggling without God's help? *Lord, I surrender to You.*

God is in every stage of the cycle. Even when you're suffering punishment, God is there because He loves you and He wants to bring you back to Himself. As a small boy, my mother would spank me because I deserved it. At the time I was sure she hated me and wanted to see me cry. Now that I'm a father and grandfather, I understand that you punish children for their own good. And you can't correct them unless you're right there to see what they do wrong. But more than seeing their infraction, you must understand what they have done and why—their motivation. Correction takes time and personal energy. You have to inconvenience your schedule before you can properly deal with them. Correction is pouring your life into their lives. You're telling them what you think is wrong and why. You're telling them what is right and why. Is that what God is doing to you? *Thank You, Lord, for correcting me with difficulties with the purpose of making me holy.*

God punished Israel, not because He was angry at them and not to hurt them. God wanted Israel to walk with Him and enjoy His presence. Isn't that always the bottom line? God wants you to know Him and walk with Him. Remember, if you're walking in close fellowship with Him, you won't be corrected by Him. You'll enjoy His fellowship. Is that your experience today? *Lord, here I am right next to You.*

My Time to Pray

*Lord, I never like being spanked by You
    But do it when I sin and run away.*

*Lord, I know You love me and care for me;
    That's why You spank me.*

Lord, I repent of my sin and come back to You;
Help me be obedient to You.

Amen.

Local Groups Remain Unconquered

SCRIPTURE: JUDGES 3:1-11

These are the nations which the Lord allowed to remain in the land. He wanted to use them to test all the Israelites who had not experienced any of the wars in Canaan. The only reason why the Lord left those nations in the land was to teach warfare to the descendants of the Israelites—those persons who had previously not fought in wars.

These are the nations: the five rulers of the Philistines, all the Canaanites (the unconquered Canaanites within Israel's territory), the people of Sidon, and the Hivites. The Hivites lived in the Lebanon mountains from Mount Baal-Hermon. Those nations were left in the land to test the Israelites. The Lord wanted to see if Israel would obey the commands that He had given to their ancestor Moses. The people of Israel settled among the Canaanites, the Hittites, the Amorites, the Perizzites, the Hivites, and the Jebusites. Then the Israelites began to marry the daughters of those nations. And the Israelites allowed their daughters to marry the sons of those people. And Israel served the gods of those people.

Othniel

The people of Israel did what was evil in the sight of the Lord. They forgot about the Lord their God. Instead, they served the Baals and the Ashtereths. The Lord was angry with Israel; He sold them into the control of Cushan-Rishathaim (meaning "Cushan, the evil one") the king of Northwest Mesopotamia who ruled over the Israelites. They served him for eight years. Then the Israelites cried out to the Lord and He raised up a deliverer for them. Othniel, the son of Kenaz (Kenaz was Caleb's younger brother), rescued the Israelites. The Spirit of the Lord came upon Othniel, and he became Israel's judge and went to war. The Lord handed over Cushan-Rishathaim, the king of Syria into Othniel's control. So the land was at peace for 40 years. Then Othniel, the son of Kenaz, died.

Judges 3

The Story of Othniel's Victory

God Uses Weak Leaders ✌ Date: 1406 B.C. ✌ Place: Northern Israel

Othniel was a mighty man among soldiers, maybe because Caleb was his hero. Remember him? Caleb was one of the 12 spies who brought back to Israel at Kadesh-Barnea a good report of the Promised Land. Ten spies doubted and put fear into the hearts of Israel so that they rebelled against God and refused to enter the Promised Land. But Caleb was a man of faith; he believed God would give Israel victory. He exhorted the people to go capture Canaan. *Lord, thank You for leaders like Caleb.*

Then at age 85, Caleb asked for Hebron, claiming, "I am as strong this day as the day when Moses first recruited me for service" (Josh. 14:11). He claimed, "I am strong...for war" (Joshua 14:11). Who wouldn't like this man's faith who said, "If the Lord is with me, then I shall drive them out" (Josh. 14:12)? *Lord, I'm glad there is no retirement in Your service. You use people as long as they are useable.*

Caleb challenged his fighters, "He that smiteth Kirjathsepher, and taketh it...I will give my daughter Achsah as his wife" (Judg. 1:12 *expanded*). Othniel, the son of Caleb's brother, challenged and took the city and got

Achsah as a reward (see Judg. 1:13). *Lord, I wonder if he knew what he was getting?*

Now Othniel did exploits in battle, but in his private life he was weak. Maybe it came from being from the younger part of the family. Maybe it was because Uncle Caleb had faith and leadership, but Othniel only enjoyed it vicariously. Maybe it was because of his domineering wife.

The wife Othniel got for bravery was just as strong as he was. When her father Caleb gave them a second-rate inheritance—maybe because Othniel was weak—his wife was not happy. She "moved Othniel to ask of her father a field" (Judg. 1:14). *Lord, if it hadn't been for Achsah, Othniel would have lived in the desert without water. If it hadn't been for her, maybe Othniel would not have conquered the enemy.*

What was the problem? Caleb gave the couple desert land without wells, streams, or springs. The Bible record looks like she "pushes" her husband to ask, but Othniel didn't ask. Then Achsah was right there when the bargaining began. It ends up that Achsah got what she demanded. Achsah asked, "Give me a blessing…give me also springs of water" (Judg. 1:15).

What were the results? "Caleb gave her the upper springs and the lower springs" (Judg. 1:15). *Lord, remind me I have not, because I ask not.*

We wouldn't say Othniel was henpecked, but it appears he married a domineering wife. A man is only henpecked when he lets it happen. Most women respect and follow a husband who takes spiritual initiative and leads a family into spirituality. *Lord, thank You for wives who make their husbands strong.*

Cushan-Rishathaim was king in Mesopotamia (names mean "land between the rivers," the Euphrates and Tigris rivers). King Cushan extended raiding parties all the way into the Holy Land. He probably sent large warring parties to collect uncollected taxes. These soldiers went from town to town and farm to farm. What riches they couldn't collect with intimidation, they seized with force.

"The children of Israel cried unto the Lord" (Judg. 3:9). The Jews were probably losing all their crops and faced starvation. Maybe young Jewish guys and girls were taken into slavery. What else could Israel do but cry unto the Lord? *Lord, I will cry to You when facing sin's slavery.*

"The Lord raised up a deliverer" (Judg. 3:9). God probably put victory upon Othniel's heart. Maybe the people remembered this "henpecked" husband from the young side of the family was a mighty warrior outside his house. The Bible uses an unusual qualifier when stating "even Othniel," suggesting Othniel's leadership was a surprise to those who knew him. *Lord, thank You for leaders who lead us to victory in spiritual battles.*

But it was not just Othniel's military skills that won the battle. "The Spirit of the Lord came upon him, and he judged Israel, and went out to war" (Judg. 3:10). Notice two things happen when Othniel was filled with the Holy Spirit. First, he judged Israel, which meant he made hard decisions, but right decisions. When you make decisions God's way, you sometimes have to decide against family and friends. Part of Othniel's judging included telling King Cushan, "No," and another part included encouraging all the people to tell the raiding parties, "No." His judgeship made him a leader. Then he led Israel to war. *Lord, teach me the power of good decisions.*

The battle was won two ways. First, God worked—"The Lord delivered King Cushan into his hands." We don't know what happened, but God turned the tide of war against King Cushan. Second, Othniel "had prevailed" which means Othniel's leadership, skill, and battle savvy won the victory.

The result, "The land had rest forty years, then Othniel died" (Judg. 3:11).

My Time to Pray

Lord, You use all kinds of people in Your service;
 Thank You for giving Achsah to make Othniel
 Into the leader You could use.

Lord, thank You for the spouse You've given me;
 Make me strong through my spouse.

Amen.

Ehud

Scripture: Judges 3:12-31

Again the people of Israel did what was evil in the sight of the Lord. So
the Lord gave Eglon, king of Moab, power to defeat Israel. This
was because of the evil that Israel did in the sight of the Lord.
Eglon also got the Ammonites and the Amalekites to join him.
Then Eglon attacked Israel and captured Jericho, the City of
Palm Trees. The people of Israel served Eglon, the king of Moab,
for 18 years. So the people of Israel cried out to the Lord, and
He raised up a deliverer to save them. *Lord, may the cycle of sin
that happened in Judges not happen in my life.*

That man was Ehud, who was left-handed. (Ehud's right hand might
have been crippled or injured.) Ehud was the son of Gera, the
Benjaminite. The people of Israel sent Ehud to give to Eglon, the
king of Moab, the payment that Eglon demanded. Ehud made a
sword for himself, a double-edged sword that was about
18 inches long. Ehud tied the sword to his right thigh under his
robe. (Ehud seemed harmless to Eglon's guards.) So Ehud
approached Eglon, the king of Moab, bringing the payment that
Eglon demanded. Now Eglon was a very fat man. After Ehud
had given the payment to Eglon, Ehud dismissed the Hebrew
men who carried it. When Ehud passed the idols near the town
of Gilgal, he turned around. Ehud said to Eglon, "O king, I have
a secret message for you." The king said to his servants, "Leave
us alone." (This royal signal meant for everyone to withdraw
from the king's presence.) Then Eglon sent all of his attendants
out of the room. Ehud went to King Eglon, who was now sitting
alone in the room of his cool roof-chamber. Ehud said, "I have a
message for you from God!" The king stood up from his throne.
Ehud used his left hand to take out the sword from his right
thigh. Then Ehud plunged the sword deep into the king's

stomach. The sword went all the way into Eglon's stomach past the handle, and it stuck out of Eglon's back. The king was so fat that his stomach closed over the blade, and Ehud could not pull the sword out. Then Ehud went out to the porch, shutting the doors to the roof-chamber and locked them behind him.

The king's servants returned soon after Ehud left, and found that the doors to the roof-chamber were locked. So they thought, "The king is relieving himself in the coolness of the room." They waited for a long time. Finally, they became worried because the king had still not opened the doors of the roof-chamber. So they got the key and unlocked the doors. When they entered, they saw their king lying on the floor dead. During the time that the servants were delaying, Ehud escaped. He passed by the idols and slipped away to Seirah.

When Ehud arrived there, he blew a trumpet (Shuphar) summoning the Jewish men to arms in the hill-country of Ephraim. The people of Israel heard it and came down from the hills. Ehud said to them, "Follow me. Let's chase them, because the Lord has given you the victory over your enemies, the people of Moab." So the Israelites came down and followed Ehud. They took control of the fording places where the Jordan River could easily be crossed. And the Israelites did not allow any Moabite to cross the Jordan River. At that time, the Israelites killed about 10,000 strong, able men from Moab. Not one Moabite man escaped back to his nation. So that day, Moab was forced to be under the rule of Israel, and there was peace in the land for 80 years. *Lord, there is strength in unity, I will unite with believers in my church to serve You.*

Shamgar

After Ehud, another judge rescued the Israelites, Shamgar, the son of
 Anath (name means warrior). Shamgar killed 600 Philistines
 (possibly the total number which occurred over Shamgar's
 career) with a sharp stick used to guide oxen. (A slender 7-foot
 long pole with a spike on one end and a knife on the other
 end.)

The Story of Ehud: God Uses the Physically Weak

Date: 1406 B.C. ~ Place: Jericho

The old Rabbis tell us that Ehud was left-handed because his right
hand was deformed or injured. He would be no threat to an armed
foe because it was thought Ehud couldn't defend himself, much less
attack. Also, Ehud was from the smallest tribe and the one perceived
weakest because they came from the youngest of the 12 sons of Jacob.
Lord, thank You for using weak people; even me.

Ehud was raised up to fight with King Eglon, from the Moabites. These
people were distant relatives of Israel because they came from Lot's
(nephew to Abraham) illicit sex with his daughter. Some have even called
it a "bastard nation" and God said a Moabite couldn't come into His presence for ten generations. Shortly we shall see how Ruth, a Moabite (11th
generation), became a godly woman who was in the line of Christ. *Lord,
thank You for grace.*

King Eglon pulled an alliance together of the Ammonites (the other bastard nation of Lot's illicit sex with his daughter) and the Amalekites. They
attacked and defeated Israel but didn't drive God's people out of God's
land. They demanded and got a large tax each year. *Lord, I know by experience that sin's wages are severe.*

Ehud apparently led a large party of Benjamites who delivered the pay-off
tax to King Eglon. Whether Ehud could use his deformed hand or not, he

was able to make a large 18˝ dagger and strap it to his right side. When the party arrived, King Eglon's guards searched the Benjamites for weapons, and according to custom, frisked them on the left side and found nothing. Maybe they didn't frisk Ehud at all because of his deformity. *Lord, teach me to be as wise as serpents, but harmless as doves.*

After delivering the "tax" to King Eglon, the party left to return home. When they got to the quarries, Ehud saw the large idol to Baal and Molek. Whereas he didn't have the courage to do something earlier, perhaps the sight of the idols in God's nation infuriated Ehud. The idol motivated him to action. He whipped around and returned to see King Eglon in Jericho. In "the hot summer time," the city of palms and its seven springs was a desirable vacation spa. King Eglon was resting in his cool, shaded summer room on the top of the house. *Lord, may I be as outraged at idolatry as was Ehud.*

When the guards told King Eglon that the man with the deformed hand had returned to see him, King Eglon must have thought, "Perhaps he has a bribe for me." When Ehud entered the room, the king commanded his guards: "Leave us alone."

"I have a message from God for you," Ehud announced.

The king got out of his seat to approach the Benjaminite, thinking maybe Ehud had money. Or the king was an idol worshiper, which meant he superstitiously worshiped all gods. Maybe he wanted to know what message the God of Israel had for him. *Lord, greed of money has destroyed many; I yield my desire of money to You.*

Ehud could have said, "Prepare to meet God;" we don't actually know what he said. But we do know Ehud reached his left hand to the dagger on his right side and plunged it deeply into the king's fat protruding from his belly.

The 18˝ dagger cut through the soft, fatty flesh and came out of Eglon's back. It plunged in so deeply, the hilt got caught up in his intestines and Ehud couldn't get it out. His bile spilled out on the floor creating such a stench the guards thought the king was relieving himself.

Ehud quickly escaped over the balcony. When the guards finally were embarrassed for waiting so long, they got a key and found their king dead. It was too late to catch Ehud the assassin. *Lord, may I be as wise as a serpent and as courageous as a lion.*

Ehud blew the shophar at Mount Ephraim. Every Jewish male knew the emergency alarm. It was a call to arms. They rallied to Ehud with sword and shield in hand, ready to rid themselves of their invaders. *Lord, thank You for the bold leadership of Ehud; may I lead with courage when You call me.*

Ehud laid out a plan to cut off the enemy, and eliminate the Moabite soldiers stationed throughout their land. Immediately, the army took control of the fords across Jordan—the only escape for the Moabite soldiers in Israel's territory. Then systematically, they killed every enemy left on their land. *Lord, You use both fighting skills and strategy to win a battle; may I follow this example.*

"At that time they struck down about ten thousand Moabites, all vigorous and strong; not a man escaped" (Judg. 3:29 NIV). *Lord, may I be decisive in dealing with sin's possession of my territory.*

My Time to Pray

Lord, You use the "division of labor" to win battles;
 Help me to learn this secret
 As I struggle to win over sin.

Lord, You reserve supernatural power to win;
 This is something only You can do.

Lord, You expect me to use my skilled physical power
 Which only I can do.

Lord, You win the battle through me, because
 "We are laborers together with God" (1 Cor. 3:9).

Amen.

Deborah's Leadership

SCRIPTURE: JUDGES 4

After Ehud died, the people of Israel again did what was evil in the
sight of the Lord. So He sold them into the control of Jabin (a
royal title), the king of Canaan, who ruled in the city of Hazor.
Sisera was Jabin's commander-in-chief. Sisera lived in Harosheth-
Haggoyim. Sisera had 900 iron chariots, and he was very cruel
to the people of Israel for 20 years. So they cried out to the
Lord for help. *Lord, Your people know the results of sin, why do
they backslide? I will be true to You.*

Deborah

Now there was a female prophetess for God named Deborah. She was
the wife of Lappidoth. She was also a judge of Israel at that
time. Deborah would always hold court under "the Palm Tree of
Deborah" between the cities of Ramah and Bethel, in the hill-
country of Ephraim. And the people of Israel were coming to her
to decide their arguments. *Lord, thank You for honest judges.*

Deborah sent a message summoning Barak, the son of Abinoam, from
the city of Kedesh, which is in the territory of Naphtali. Deborah
told Barak, "This is what the Lord, the God of Israel, commands
you: 'Go and mobilize 10,000 men of Naphtali and Zebulun.
Go, lead them to Mount Tabor. God will cause Sisera, the
commander-in-chief of Jabin's army, to come to you, luring him,
his army, and his chariots to the Kishon River. God will hand
Sisera over to you there.'" (In normal weather, the Kishon was
only a dried up riverbed, a wadi. However, God overwhelmed

Sisera's chariots with a huge flash flood [see Judg. 5:4,21].) *God, You use atmospheric calamities to win military battles. Thank You for perfect timing.*

Then Barak said to Deborah, "I will go, if you will go with me. But if you will not go with me, then I won't go." Deborah answered, "Of course I will go with you. However, you will not get credit for the victory. The Lord will defeat Sisera through the power of a woman" (namely, Jael). So, Deborah went with Barak to Kedesh. Barak summoned the troops of Zebulun and Naphtali to Kedesh. From them, Barak gathered 10,000 men to follow him. Deborah also went with Barak. *Lord, thank You for those who prepared for victory.*

In the past, Heber the Kenite had separated from the other Kenite people. The Kenites were descendants of Hobab, Moses' father-in-law. Heber had put up his tent by the big tree in Zaanannim, near Kedesh. Someone told Sisera that Barak had gone up to Mount Tabor. So Sisera summoned all of his 900 iron chariots and all his men with him. They went from Harosheth-Haggoyim to the Kishon River.

Then Deborah told Barak: "Get up, today is the day that the Lord has put Sisera into your control. You know that the Lord has already cleared the way for you." So Barak led the 10,000 men down from Mount Tabor. During Barak's attack, the Lord threw Sisera's army and charioteers into a panic. (The horses probably became very frightened by lightning and thunder and stampeded.) Barak and his soldiers started hacking away with their swords. Sisera left his own chariot and ran away on foot. *Lord, thank You for courageous men who didn't panic.*

Then Barak and his men chased Sisera's chariots and army to Harosheth-Haggoyim. They used their swords to kill all of Sisera's army. Not even one of them was left alive. Now Sisera fled on foot to the tent of Jael. She was the wife of Heber the Kenite. Heber the Kenite's household was at peace with Jabin, the king of Hazor. Jael went out to meet Sisera, saying to him, "Sir, come into my tent. Don't be afraid!" So Sisera went into Jael's tent, and she covered him with a heavy rug. Sisera said to Jael, "I am very thirsty. Please give me some water to drink." So she opened a leather bag containing milk, and she gave him a drink. Then she covered him up. Then Sisera said to Jael, "Go stand at the entrance to the tent. If anyone comes by and asks you, 'Is a man here?' then say: 'No!'"

But Jael, the wife of Heber, took a tentpeg and grabbed a hammer and quietly crept up on Sisera, since he was exhausted and was sound asleep. Then she drove the tent peg right through the side of Sisera's head and pounded it into the ground. And so, Sisera died. Later, while still chasing Sisera, Barak came to Jael's tent. She went out to meet Barak and said to him, "Come, I will show you the man you are looking for." So Barak entered the tent, and saw Sisera lying there dead—with the tent peg through his head. On that day, God defeated Jabin, the king of Canaan, in front of the Israelites. The Israelites pressed harder and harder against Jabin, the king of Canaan, finally destroying him.

Judges 4

The Story of Deborah

Date 1336 B.C. ☙ Place: Ramah

The Spirit of God rested on Deborah, both a prophetess and judge. People recognized her wisdom and fairness. They came from all over to get her to settle their disputes. Today western judges do their legal work at the bar usually in a local building, but in the ancient Mideast, judges did their work in the open, usually near the town gate. *Lord, I know Christians will be judged at the Bema Throne for their good works, and the unsaved will be judged at the Great White Judgment Throne.*

But Deborah worked under the palm tree named Deborah. Some say she chose that place because it was the same as her name. Others say Deborah was named after the tree; maybe she was born there and was named for the geographical location.

Deborah was married, but her husband was inconsequential to the story as were her children, if she had any.

The original Deborah was a nursemaid for Rachel, wife of Jacob. When they were moving back into the Promised Land, Deborah died and was buried under a palm tree in the north that eventually became known for her (see Gen. 35:8). The second Deborah was a judge who held court under this tree.

Deborah, the judge, called for Barak and spoke prophetically to him the Word of God, "I the Lord command you to call 10,000 fighting men to Mount Tabor." This mountain stood by itself in the "Valley of Armageddon" with steep sides and a flat top approximately one mile across. A perfect place to assemble an army because it was near a perfect battle ground, yet the steep slopes gave them an advantage if attacked. God told Barak,

"I will deliver the enemy into your hands."

The Canaanites were punishing Israel because Joshua had driven them from their northern strongholds. Punishments were probably unrealistic taxes, forced labor, and slavery at the whim of Jabin, king of the Canaanites, and Sisera, general of his army. Their army had 900 chariots with iron wheels. When they attacked Israel in battle, defenders placed logs or rocks in their way to splinter wooden chariot wheels. But iron wheels bumped over an obstacle and crushed an opposing soldier. No wonder Israel cried unto the Lord (see Judg. 4:3). *Lord, I trust You for victory because You know the tricks of the enemy.*

God promised Barak victory as He spoke through Deborah, "I will lure Sisera into the River Kishon." Barak may have thought that was not much of a promise because this river was a wadi, a dry riverbed. No obstacle for iron wheels. Did Barak realize that God would send a thunder storm at the beginning of the battle to neutralize the iron wheels? Probably not because he insisted on Deborah going with him to the battle. *Lord, I will trust You because You not only know the future, You manipulate the future to accomplish Your will.*

Maybe Barak wanted Deborah as a "good luck" charm in battle. Maybe he wanted a word from God to help him with strategy in battle. Barak doesn't sound like a strong leader when he begs a woman to go along with him. Deborah responds,

"I will surely go with you."

But because of Barak's timidity, Deborah chastens him with this prediction, "You have not chosen the road of honor, because the Lord will deliver Sisera into the hands of a woman." Because Barak usually outthinks himself, he probably thought Deborah would claim victory for the battle. He didn't know that God would use the woman Jael. *Lord, You use both men and women in Your work.*

Heber, a Kenite had pitched his tent near where the battle would take place. Heber was a Kenite, from the family of Moses' father-in-law. Heber had broken relations with Israel and aligned himself with the Canaanites—probably for safety's sake because they were in power. But blood runs thicker than water, and when a pinch came, Heber's wife would align herself with the Lord God of Israel. *Lord, I'm continually surprised where I find Your servants.*

To start the battle, Deborah commanded Barak, "Get up, attack the enemy, charge down Tabor." Barak may have thought a woman doesn't understand battle strategy, "It's hard for iron wheels to charge uphill. The army in the height has the advantage. If our army goes down on the valley floor, we've given up our advantage. Iron wheels will crush us."

To Barak's credit, he charged down Tabor to meet the enemy on a level field of battle. But the field was not level. God's timing is perfect; a thunderstorm broke over the valley of Armageddon. A flash flood drove the river over its banks, and the iron wheels stuck in the mud. The advantage went to Israel with flashing swords, and righteous indignation. God's soldiers swarmed over the incapacitated iron wheels and Sisera's army fled in panic.

Sisera jumped from his chariot and began to run. Barak and his men pursued the frightened general. Maybe the downpours obscured their vision, or maybe a scared Sisera outran Barak; but Sisera got away. *Lord, when people run from You, they don't get very far.*

Sisera ran into the encampment of Heber and he must have felt safe because the Canaanites and Heber had a "peace pact." Jael met him:

"Come into my tent," Jael invited the exhausted, wet Sisera in out of the rain.

"I'm thirsty," Sisera pleaded, so Jael gave him a leather bottle of milk. Sisera must have thought he was lucky to get nourishment for his depleted strength.

"Watch the door," Sisera told the woman, "if anyone comes looking for me, tell them there is no man inside your tent."

An exhausted Sisera went to sleep in a warm dry tent, and Jael covered him with a blanket. With the sound of rain beating on the tent, the last thing in Sisera's mind was his luck in finding Jael's tent. But that was not the last thing to enter Sisera's head.

Jael got a long tent peg and mallet and crept softly to where Sisera slept. The last thing in Sisera's head was that tent peg, for Jael pounded it through his temple into the ground. Outwardly her family had an alliance with the Canaanites, but inwardly her allegiance was to God, for she knew the vengeance they reaped on her kinsmen. *Lord, I will never doubt the vengeance of a woman who is committed to righteousness.*

When Barak finally came running by the tent, Jael met him and said, "I'll show you the man you're searching for." She showed him Sisera, nailed to the ground with a tent peg through his temple.

The battle continued until the army of Israel pursued and destroyed King Jabin of the Canaanites. Then Israel in the north had peace. *Lord, one day the last battle will be over. It will be another—different—battle on the plain of Armageddon. I look forward to that day.*

My Time to Pray

Lord, You give us victory in many different ways;
    Teach me to trust the methods You use.

You gave Israel a victory through Barak, and
    Deborah the judge, and Jael a distant relative.

Lord, You work Your mighty mysterious ways
    Through little things like a tent peg;
    Teach me to trust the details of Your work.

Amen.

The Song of Deborah and Barak

SCRIPTURE: JUDGES 5

On that day, Deborah and Barak sang this song (perhaps antiphonally):

"The leaders freely led Israel;
>   The people gladly volunteered to follow,
>   Praise the Lord.

Listen, O you pagan kings (Note, Israel had no king at this time;)
>   Pay attention, you heathen rulers.

I myself will sing to the Lord;
>   I will sing praises to the Lord, the God of Israel.

O Lord, in the past, you came forth from Seir;
>   You marched from the region of Edom,
>   And the earth shook.
>>   The skies poured down its rain;
>>   Yes, the clouds dropped water (They are describing
>>   the thunderstorm and flash flood that provided
>>   victory over the Canaanites.)

The mountains shook in the presence of the Lord;
>   Yes, even Mount Sinai did so in the presence of the Lord, the
>   God of Israel!

In the days of Shamgar, the son of Anath,
>   In the days of Jael, the main roads were empty.

Travelers used the crooked side paths. (Evidence the country was occu-
>   pied by a foreign invader, locals were afraid to travel openly.)

The towns of Israel were abandoned,
> They were all empty until I came up;
> I, Deborah, arose like a mother in Israel.

Israel had chosen to follow new gods,
> Then war came to our gates;
> None could find a shield or a spear (foreign masters would not let them possess shields or spears).

Among the 40,000 men in Israel.
> My heart went out to the commanders of Israel.

The people gladly volunteered when challenged;
> Praise the Lord.

You persons who ride on white donkeys (only rich people could afford them),
> And who sit on expensive saddle blankets,
> And you who walk along the road, sing.

Sing louder than the singers gathered around the watering holes.

That's where they tell about the righteous victories of the Lord;
> The righteous deeds of His leaders in Israel.

Then the Lord's people came down to the city gates;
> "Wake up, wake up, O Deborah
> Wake up, wake up; sing a song.

Get up, O Barak,
> Lead your captives away, O son of Abinoam."

Then the remaining patriotic ones came down to their leaders;
> The Lord's people marched down for Him, ready to fight.

They came down from Ephraim in the mountains into the valley,
> Behind you, O tribe of Benjamin with your people.

The commanders descended from the clan of Machir;
>And from the tribe of Zebulun came those men who
>lead with the staff of an officer.

And the princes of Issachar were with Deborah;
>Yes, the people of Issachar were loyal to Barak, too,
>They followed him into the valley.

However, among the ranks of the tribe of Reuben,
>There were great searchings of the heart (The Reubenites
>couldn't make up their minds about whether to support their
>Hebrew brothers in their war against the Canaanites. The
>Reubenites decided not to come.)
>Why did you stay home among the campfires?
>Was it to hear the shepherds whistling for the flocks?

Among the ranks of the tribe of Reuben,
>There were great searchings of the heart.

The people of Gilead stayed east of the Jordan River;
>O people of Dan, why did you linger beside the ships?

The people of Asher remained at the seacoast;
>They stayed at the shore.

But Zebulun are a people who jeopardized their very lives;
>So did the people of Naphtali on the battlefield.

The pagan kings came and fought;
>At that time, the kings of Canaan fought at Taanach,

Beside the stream of the Kishon River;
>But they didn't carry away any silver; no plunder.

The stars from heaven fought
>From their paths;
>They fought against Sisera.

The Kishon River swept Sisera's men away,
> That old river, the Kishon River
> Will march on mightily!

Then the hoofs of the horses did beat from the galloping,
> Sisera's mighty stallions galloping.

Put a curse on Meroz (A village somewhere within the territories of
> Issachar and Naphtali in the path of the Canaanite fugitives, but
> they refused to help their Hebrew brothers),
> Said the Angel of the Lord,
> Bitterly curse the people who live there.

Why? Because they did not come to help the Lord,
> To help the Lord among the soldiers.

Jael, the wife of Heber, the Kenite, is more blessed than other women;
> She should be blessed more than all the women who live in
> tents.

Sisera asked for water,
> But Jael gave him milk.

In a bowl fit for a king,
> She brought him cream.

Then Jael took a tent peg in one hand,
> And her right hand reached for a workman's hammer.

And she hammered Sisera;
> She smashed his head;
> She pierced and crushed the side of his head.

Between Jael's feet he sank;
> He fell. He lay.

Between her feet, he sank. He fell;
> Where Sisera sank, there he fell—dead.

(The scene changes here to the Canaanite palace where Sisera's
worried mother awaits her son who was delayed by his battle
with the Israelites.)

Sisera's mother looked out through her window;
    She peered through the lattice.

'Yes,' she asked, 'Why is Sisera's chariot so late in coming?
    Why are the sounds of the horses of his chariots delayed?'

Of her female attendants, the wise ones answer her;
    'Yes,' Sisera's mother thinks to herself over and over:
    'Surely the Canaanite soldiers are finding loot
    And dividing it up among themselves,
    And it takes time.

A girl or two for every soldier;
    Perhaps Sisera is taking pieces of gorgeous cloth.

Maybe they are even taking pieces of rich, embroidered cloth;
    Two such garments for the necks of the victors?'

Let all your enemies perish this way, O One Who is the Lord;
    But let all the people who love You
    Shine like the sun at its hottest."

So there was peace from war in the land for 40 years.

God's Call to Gideon

SCRIPTURE: JUDGES 6

Nevertheless, the Israelites did what was evil in the sight of the Lord. So
the Lord permitted the people of Midian (a large section of
Arabs who called themselves "Ishmaelites," or desert raiders) to
control Israel for seven years. The Midianites oppressed Israel, so
the Israelites hid their food in shelters in the hill-country. They
also hid personally in caves and strongholds. Whenever the
Israelites planted crops, the Midianites, the Amalekites, and the
other eastern peoples (marauding Arabs) would attack them.
Those people camped against them on the land and destroyed
the crops that the Israelites had planted. They did this in the
Gaza territory. They left nothing for Israel to eat—no sheep, no
cattle, and no donkeys. *Lord, Israel got the punishment they
deserved for compromising with idolatry and the world.*

When they came up and camped out, they brought all their tents and
animals with them. They invaded in large numbers, like swarms
of locusts. It was impossible to count all of the people and their
camels. These people just came into the land of Israel to destroy
it. Therefore, Israel became very poor because of the Midianites.
So the Israelites cried out to the Lord for help. *Lord, may I call
out to You before You punish me for my sin.*

When Israel cried out to the Lord for help because of the Midianite
oppression, the Lord sent a man, a prophet, to them. The
prophet said, "This is what the Lord, the God of Israel, says: I
brought you up from Egypt out of a household of slaves. I rescued you from the control of the people of Egypt. And in
Canaan, I have also rescued you from all those who oppressed

you. As you advanced, I drove them out. And I gave their land to you. Then I said to you, "I am the Lord your God. You may settle in the land of the Amorites but you must not worship their gods." *Lord, I will obey.*

"However, you did not obey Me." The Angel of the Lord came and sat down underneath the oak tree at Ophrah. The tree belonged to Joash, who was one of the Abiezrite people (descendants of Manasseh). Gideon, the son of Joash, was separating out some wheat from the chaff in a winepress. (This was a very small quantity of grain that Gideon was threshing in a small confined area.) He did this to hide the wheat so that the Midianites would not discover it. The Angel of the Lord appeared to Gideon and said to him, "The Lord is with you, O strong warrior." *Lord, may I recognize You when You come to me.*

Then Gideon said, "What? (The words seemed a mockery.) Sir, if the Lord were with us, then why are so many troubles finding us? Our ancestors used to tell us over and over again that God did such awesome deeds. They told us how the Lord brought them out of Egypt. Where are those miracles now? No, the Lord has abandoned us. He has allowed the Midianites to control us."

The Lord turned to Gideon and said, "You have the strength to deliver the people of Israel. Go and save them from the control of the Midianites. Have I sent you?" *Lord, send me.*

But Gideon answered, "But, my Lord, how could I save Israel? Look, my clan is the weakest one in the tribe of Manasseh. And I am the least important member of my family."

The Lord answered him, "Because I will be with you. You must strike down the Midianites as if they were only one man." *Lord, thank You for taking the least and using them for Your glory. Use me.*

Then Gideon said to the Lord, "If You are pleased with me, then perform a miracle or a sign. Prove to me that You are the One who is truly speaking with me. Please stay here until I come back. I will bring my food offering and sacrifice it in front of You." (If He accepted the sacrificial gift, then it would be conclusive proof that this appearance was God.) The Lord said, "I will wait here until you come back." *Lord, take away my doubt; may I believe in You without external proofs.*

So Gideon went and prepared a young goat. He also took one ephah of flour and made some bread without any yeast (unleavened bread). Then he put the meat into a basket. And Gideon put the broth from the meat into a pot. He brought them out and offered them to Him under the oak tree. *Lord, I also sacrifice to You.*

The Angel of the Lord said to Gideon, "Take the meat and the bread without yeast, and put them on top of this rock. Then pour the broth on them." And Gideon did so. The Angel of the Lord had a stick in His hand. He touched the meat and unleavened bread with the tip of the stick, then fire jumped up out of the rock (indicating divine acceptance). It burned up the meat and the bread completely. And the Angel of the Lord vanished. *Lord, my sacrifice to You is Jesus on the Cross.*

When Gideon realized that the Man was the Angel of the Lord, Gideon cried out, "Alas, O Lord God, I have seen the Angel of the Lord face to face." But the Lord told Gideon, "Don't be afraid, you will not die." So Gideon built an altar there to worship the Lord. Gideon named that altar "Yahweh-Shalom" ("the Lord is peace"). It is still at Ophrah today, where the Abiezrites live. *Lord, I worship when You come to me.*

That same night, the Lord talked to Gideon: "Take the young bull that belongs to your father and the second bull that is seven years old. Tear down your father's altar to Baal. And cut down the pole of the Asherah idol which is next to it." *Lord, I will clean up sin in my own life before I deal with sin in the lives of others.*

"Then you must build an altar to the Lord your God on top of this mound. Carefully lay out stones, then take the second bull and kill it, and offer it as a whole burnt offering on this altar to Me. Use the wood from the Asherah pillar which you will have just cut down to make the fire." *Lord, it takes courage to stand for You against my family.*

So, Gideon got ten servants, and did what the Lord had told him to do. But Gideon was afraid that his own family and the men of the city might see him do this. So Gideon did it at night. The men of the city got up the next morning, and behold, they saw that the altar for Baal had been demolished, and they also saw that the Asherah idol beside it had been cut down. They saw the altar which had been built and the second bull that had been sacrificed up on it. The men of the city asked each other, "Who did this?" They asked many questions, carefully investigating to find out who had done these things. Someone said, "Gideon, the son of Joash, did this deed." So the men of the city said to Joash, "Bring out your son, he must die. He has demolished the altar of Baal. He has also cut down the Asherah idol which was next to it."

But Joash spoke to all those who confronted him, saying, "Are you pleading Baal's case? Are you trying to save Baal? Anyone who takes Baal's side will be executed by morning. If Baal is a god, let him fight for himself. It is his altar that has been demolished." So on that day, Gideon was nicknamed "Jerub-Baal." (The name means "Baal-fighter".) That is what they named Gideon because he had demolished Baal's altar. *Lord, the world will always attack me when I take a stand for You.*

Now, all the Midianites, Amalekites, and eastern peoples had joined themselves together at the ford of the Jordan River, and camped in the valley of Jezreel. But the Spirit of the Lord entered Gideon, he blew a trumpet (shophar) to call the Abiezrites to follow him. *Lord, I want the Spirit of God on my life.*

Gideon Summons Jewish Soldiers

Gideon sent messengers to all the territory of Manasseh, calling them to arms. Gideon also sent messengers to the tribes of Asher, Zebulun, and Naphtali, who also went up to meet Gideon and his men. Then Gideon said to the Lord, "You have said that You are about to use me as an instrument to save Israel. I will put a fleece of wool on the ground where we thresh the wheat. Let the dew be only on the wool, but let all of the ground around it be dry. Then I will know what you said is true—that you will be using me to save Israel." That is exactly what happened. Gideon got up early the next morning and squeezed the fleece and wrung out water. He got enough water from the wool to fill one bowl. *Lord, I shall not use "fleece" to determine Your will; I shall find it in Scripture.*

Then Gideon said to God, "Please don't be angry with me. Let me ask for just one more sign. This time, please cause the fleece to be dry and let the ground be covered with dew." That night, that is the very thing God did. The fleece was dry, (this sign was even more convincing, because it is the nature of wool fleeces to attract and retain moisture) but the ground surrounding it was all wet with dew. *Lord, I don't need signs; I see Your commands to me in Scripture.*

Judges 6

The Story of Gideon

Date: 1249 B.C. ⌒ Place: Orphrah

And the Angel of the Lord appeared to him, and said to him, "The Lord is with you, you mighty man of valor!" Gideon said to Him, "O my lord, if the Lord is with us, why then has all this happened to us? And where are all His miracles which our fathers told us about, saying, 'Did not the Lord bring us up from Egypt?' But now the Lord has forsaken us and delivered us into the hands of the Midianites" (Judges 6:12-13).

Has God ever told you to do something, but you didn't do it, because you thought you were inadequate? When you were praying, a great idea came to you, but you never acted on it because you thought you couldn't do it. There may have been many reasons why you did nothing! You didn't have enough money, enough leadership ability, or enough courage. You immediately thought failure, not success. When God wanted you to move forward, you couldn't move at all. *Lord, that's me.*

God had a great job for Gideon to do, but he was filled with doubt and insecurity. The Lord appeared to Gideon, and he didn't even know it was God. The Lord greeted Gideon to build up his self-confidence, "The Lord is with you, because you are a mighty man of courage." But Gideon's doubt controlled his answer, "If God is with me, where are all His miracles He did for Israel in bringing them out of the desert? If God is with me, why have the Midianites conquered us and now they take all our food?"

Have you ever doubted God because you couldn't see a miracle? Are you skeptical because luck has turned against you? If Gideon understood Israel was in economic captivity because of her sin, he wouldn't have complained. If Gideon understood how God worked, maybe he would have understood God wanted to use him. How about you? Are you in difficulty because you don't know how God works, or you've forgotten what He can do? When God comes to you with a task, don't immediately look to your weakness or your doubt. *Lord, I will immediately look to You.*

God told Gideon, "You shall save Israel" (Judg. 6:14). But Gideon still doubted, "If I shall save Israel, show me a sign." Do you look for outward proof to verify the inward voice of God? It's as though Gideon said, "Show me a miracle and I'll obey you." Isn't that unbelief? *Lord, I believe; help my unbelief.*

Gideon brought a young goat as a blood sacrifice and the other things required in a peace offering to God. He spread the meat and cakes on a rock. Then the miraculous happened. The Angel of the Lord touched the sacrifice and instantly a fire consumed them. Then the Lord disappeared in the flame and Gideon's unbelief kicked in again. Gideon cried, "I've seen the Lord and I'll die." But God spoke to tell Gideon he wouldn't die. Gideon built an altar on the spot and called it Jehovah-Shalom—*the Lord, my peace.* Have you made peace with God? *Lord, let Your peace control my life.*

Still Gideon was afraid to serve the Lord. That night under the cover of darkness, Gideon cut down the grove of trees on the tallest hill of his father's farm. The trees surrounded an altar to Baal, the false god of the heathen. Gideon destroyed the altar. Then Gideon took his father's bull—usually a farmer had only one—and sacrificed it to the Lord. The next morning the neighbors were incensed; they wanted to kill Gideon. The neighbors worshiped Baal the fertility god because they thought Baal would give them prosperity. They thought Baal would protect them. Even though Gideon's father was a Baal-worshiper, he had enough common sense to say, "If Baal is a god, let him protect himself."

Gideon tried to serve the Lord under the cover of darkness, but he was still a coward. He was afraid of what others would think of him. Is that you? Do you serve the Lord quietly, out of public view, only in your prayer closet? *Lord, I will tell others.*

My Time to Pray

Lord, forgive me when I doubt as Gideon;
But it's so easy to doubt
When I get my eyes off You.

Lord, I'll keep my spiritual eyes on You;
I'll follow when You lead,
I'll go where You want me to go.

Amen.

God Defeats the Midianites

SCRIPTURE: JUDGES 7

Early in the morning, Jerub-Baal (Gideon) and all his army set up their
camp beside Harod Spring. The Midianite army was north of
him, in the valley at the bottom of the hill called Moreh (about
four miles away). Then the Lord said to Gideon, "You have too
many men for me to give you a victory over the Midianites. I do
not want the Israelites to brag, thinking that they saved themselves." *Lord, may I see only You.*

"So now, make this announcement to your army: 'Anyone who is trem-
bling or fearful may leave Mount Gilead, you may go back home
now'" (see Deut. 20:8). Then 22,000 men went back home. But
10,000 men remained.

Then the Lord said to Gideon, "There are still too many men. Take the
men down to the water, and I will separate them for you there.
If I say about one: 'This man will go with you,' then he will go
with you. But if I say, 'That one will not go with you,' then he
may not go." So Gideon led the men down to the water. The
Lord said to him, "Those who put their mouths down to the
water (he assumes a defenseless position) will be in one group.
But those who bend down on one knee and scoop up the water
to drink (he is alertly aware of anyone who might attack him
while drinking water) will be in the other group. Separate them
into those two categories." There were about 300 men who used
their cupped hands to bring water to their mouths. All the rest
of the men got down on their knees to drink water like a dog.
Then the Lord said to Gideon, "I will use those 300 men who
cupped water to save you and give you victory over the

Midianites. Tell everyone else to go home." *Lord, help me learn that Your ways are different from man's ways.*

So Gideon sent everybody else home, but he kept the 300 men. *Lord, may I always be ready to serve You. May I always be on guard against sin.*

Then Gideon got clay pots and trumpets (shophar) for his soldiers. Now the Midianite camp was in the valley, below where Gideon was located.

That night, the Lord spoke to Gideon saying, "Get up, go down and attack the camp of the Midianites, because I have given you victory over them. However, if you are still afraid to descend upon the camp, take your young assistant, Purah, with you and go down there. You will overhear what they are saying. After that, you will get the courage to go down and attack the Midianite camp." So Gideon and Purah, his young helper, decided to go down to the edge of the front lines of the Midianite camp. The Midianites, Amalekites, and all the eastern peoples were camped along the valley. There were so many of them they were like a swarm of locusts. They had more camels than one could count—they were as many as the grains of sand on the beach. When Gideon got there, he overheard a man telling his friend about a dream that he just had, saying: "I just dreamed that a loaf of barley bread tumbled into the camp of Midian, and hit the main tent with such force that the tent turned over and collapsed." The man's friend said, "Your dream can only mean one thing—it is about the sword of Gideon, the son of Joash, a man of Israel. God will let Gideon gain a victory over Midian and the whole army." When Gideon overheard this dream and what it meant, he worshiped God. Then Gideon and his helper returned to the camp of Israel. He called out to his soldiers, "Get up, because the Lord has already defeated the army of Midian for you." *Lord, thank You for assurance.*

Then Gideon divided his 300 men into three groups. He gave a trumpet and an empty clay pot to each man. There was a burning torch inside each clay pot. Then Gideon told his men, "Watch me, and do what I do. When I get to the edge of the Midianite camp, do exactly what I do. We'll surround their entire camp. Then I, and everyone with me, will blow our trumpets. When we blow our trumpets, you blow your trumpets. Then shout, 'For the Lord and for Gideon.'" (Upon hearing the trumpets and the battle cries, any opposing soldier would be expecting an immediate assault. When 300 trumpets blasted from all direction, it is no wonder that panic ensued in the Midianite camp.)

So Gideon and the 100 men who were with him went to the edge of the camp of the Midianites. They got there right after the Midianites had changed guards. (It was during the middle watch of the night, about 12:00 P.M.). Then Gideon and his men blew their trumpets and shattered the clay pots that were in their hands. All three groups of Gideon's men blew their trumpets and shattered their clay pots at the same time. They held the flaming torches in their left hands and the trumpets in their right hands. They shouted: "A sword for the Lord and for Gideon." Each of Gideon's men stayed in his position around the Midianite camp.

But inside the camp, all the Midianite men began shouting and rushing around in panic, wanting to escape. When Gideon's 300 men blew their trumpets, the Lord caused all the Midianites to fight each other with their swords—the whole camp. The Midianite army ran away to the town of Beth-Shittah, toward the town of Zererah. They ran as far as the border of the town of Abel-Meholah. It is near the town of Tabbath. Then the men of Israel from the tribes of Naphtali, Asher, and all the men of Manasseh were called out to continue chasing the Midianites. Gideon sent messengers throughout all the hill-country of Ephraim, saying,

"Come down to attack the Midianites. Capture the fords of the Jordan River ahead of them, as far as Beth-Barah. Do this before the Midianites can get to the river and cross it." So the Ephraimites took control of the water fords of the Jordan River as far as Beth-Barah. And they continued to chase after the Midianites. The men of Ephraim captured two princes of Midian named Oreb and Zeeb. They executed Oreb at "The Rock of Oreb." And killed Zeeb at Zeeb's Winepress. They cut off the heads of Oreb and Zeeb and brought them to Gideon who was next to the Jordan River. *Lord, teach me the lesson of courage and unity.*

Judges 7

The Story of Gideon's Victory

Date: 1249 B.C. ⌒ Place: Hill of Moach

Gideon had a test for God. He prayed, "I am going to put the wool of a lamb out tonight." He told God, "If You are going to use me, let the fleece be soaking wet in the morning." The next morning, Gideon squeezed water out of the wool. Gideon must have figured the porous wool attracted moisture. So he prayed, "Tonight, Lord, keep the wool dry, but let the sand around it be wet. The next morning the wool was dry. This should have encouraged Gideon to go attack the Midianites. Are you like Gideon? Do you think up one test after another to see if God is with you, or if God will use you? But your problem is internal; it's not things or circumstances. The problem is you—it's unbelief. *Lord, help me overcome unbelief.*

Gideon still was not yet convinced God would use him. He had another test. Gideon marched his soldiers to the creek for a drink. Some of the men got down on all fours and lapped the water with their mouth, just like an animal. The other men knelt down on one knee and scooped water to their mouths with their hands on their swords. These men were alert and ready for battle because the enemy was nearby. God chose these. God didn't choose the men with their faces in the water. Some say they were worshiping the water. Others say they were like "dogs." God chose to use the 300 men who drank with their hands on their weapons. *Lord, I'm ready to be used.*

What will you do when you are tested? Some days God tests you, and you don't even know it. So the answer is to be faithful to God all the time in every way, especially the small ways. *Lord, I see You in the details of life.*

It's one thing to be tested by God, but it's entirely another thing to test God. God called Gideon, but the young man was not sure God could use him. So Gideon put God to several tests. What does that say about Gideon? Doesn't that say he was motivated by unbelief? Doesn't that say Gideon had trouble accepting himself? He was probably an introvert and lacked self-confidence. Is that you? Do you lack confidence? Are you too introverted? Don't measure a task by your ability; rather, think what God can do. Learn from God. Walk with God. Trust God. *Lord, take away my doubts.*

If you're drawn inward like Gideon, remember what God did with Gideon and his 300 men. God can use you, because He delights to use people who trust in Him. *Lord, I'll trust You.*

In the middle of the night each of the 300 soldiers took a trumpet in one hand and a torch burning in a pitcher in the other hand. Their sword was in the sheath. God was going to win this battle, not these 300 fighting men with their flashing swords. At a given signal, each of the 300 men broke the pitchers, waved the torches, and blew the trumpets. To the enemy, it sounded like Gideon's army was attacking. The enemy didn't know how many were charging in the darkness. They didn't know who was beside them. They killed the closest thing that moved. God gave Gideon a great victory; the enemy slaughtered itself.

When God called Gideon, the young man struggled with the call. Gideon was not sure God could use him. Are you like Gideon, filled with self-doubt? Look to God's call, "He who calls you is faithful, who also will do it" (1 Thess. 5:24). *Lord, I answer Your call.*

My Time to Pray

Lord, I trust You to give me victory over the enemy
Even when I don't know how it'll come.

Lord, I want to serve You with all my heart;
Use me in Your service.

Amen.

Gideon Pursues Zebah and Zalmunna

Scripture: Judges 8

The men of Ephraim asked Gideon, "Why did you treat us this way? (The Ephraimites were upset because they had not shared in the glory of Gideon's victory over the hated Midianites. The territory of the Ephraimites was in the mountains, and the Midianites had not raided them.) Why didn't you call us when you first went out to fight against Midian?" They criticized Gideon sharply, but Gideon answered, "I have not done as well as what you accomplished. The small part that you did was far better than everything that my people of Abiezer did. God allowed you to capture Oreb and Zeeb, and princes of Midian. What was I able to do compared to you?" When the men of Ephraim heard Gideon's answer, they were not as angry anymore. *Lord, teach me to be as wise as Gideon, to emphasize what others did and minimize what I do.*

Then Gideon and his 300 men came to the Jordan River. They were exhausted but they kept chasing the Midianites across to the other side. Gideon said to the men of Succoth (this town was on the other side of the Jordan River), "Please give my soldiers some bread. I am still chasing Zebah and Zalmunna, the kings of Midian." But the leaders of Succoth said, "Why should we give your soldiers bread? You haven't caught Zebah and Zalmunna yet." (These local Jewish brothers were still afraid that those roving Midianite sheiks might not be defeated.) *Lord, help me always to do right and never be afraid of reprisals.*

Then Gideon said, "Alright, the Lord will indeed help me capture Zebah and Zalmunna. After that, I will thrash your skin with thorns and briers from the desert." Gideon left Succoth and went to the city of Peniel. He asked the men there for food also. But the men of Peniel gave him the same answer as the men of Succoth. So Gideon said the same thing to the men of Peniel, "After I come back in peace from the next victory, I'm going to demolish this tower."

Zebah and Zalmunna and their army were in the city of Karkor, their army still numbered about 15,000 men. They were all that was left of the army of the eastern peoples. Already 120,000 soldiers of that army had been killed. Then Gideon went up by the caravan route, east of Nobah and Jogbehah, striking at the Midianite army in surprise raids. (Apparently, Gideon circled around to the east of the fleeing Midianites and surprised them at night.) Gideon attacked their army when they did not expect it. Zebah and Zalmunna, the two kings of Midian, ran away; but Gideon continued chasing them, and captured them both. *Lord, thank You for giving Your servants wisdom in war.*

Gideon and his men caused that entire army to panic. Then Gideon and his men returned from the battle before the sun came up. (Gideon's small army had attacked the Midianite army at night.) Gideon captured a young man from Succoth and asked him some questions. The young man wrote down the names of 77 men who were the leaders and elders of Succoth. Then Gideon came to the city of Succoth and said to the men of that city, "Look, here are Zebah and Zalmunna. You made fun of me by saying: 'Why should we give bread to your exhausted men? You haven't caught Zebah and Zalmunna yet!'" Then Gideon took the elders of that city, and he thrashed them with thorns and briers from the desert. Gideon also demolished the tower of Peniel. Then he killed the leading men in that city.

Then Gideon spoke to Zebah and Zalmunna, saying, "You killed some Jewish men on Mount Tabor. What kind of men were they?"

Zebah and Zalmunna answered, "They were like you. Each one of them seemed like a prince." Gideon said, "Well, those were my brothers, the sons of my own mother. I solemnly swear if you had spared them, I would not kill you." (Here Gideon is carrying out the duty of a go'el [see Num. 35:12; Deut. 19:6]. They had murdered his blood-kin [compare Num. 35:19,27].) Then Gideon turned to Jether, his oldest son, and said, "Kill them." But Jether was only a boy and was afraid to do it. So Jether did not pull out his sword. Then Zebah and Zalmunna said to Gideon, "Come on, you kill us yourselves. It takes a man to do a man's job" (literally, "As the man is, so is his strength"). So Gideon got up and killed Zebah and Zalmunna. Then Gideon took the decorations off the necks of their camels. (These were prizes of victory, crescent-like plates of gold which were suspended from the necks of the camels of the Midianites.) *Lord, life is serious and sin has consequences. Teach me to be thorough.*

Gideon Refuses to Be Their King

The men of Israel said to Gideon, "You have saved us from the Midianites. Therefore, please be our ruler. We want you, your son, and your grandson to rule over us." But Gideon told them, "The Lord will be your Ruler. I will not rule over you. And my son will not rule over you, either." He said to them, "I do request this thing though—that each of you gives me a gold earring from among the things you captured in the fighting." The Ishmaelite men wore gold earrings. So the soldiers of Israel said to Gideon, "We will gladly give you whatever you want." So they spread out a robe on the ground. Then each man threw a captured earring onto the robe. The gold earrings weighed about 43 pounds, not including the weight of the other donations which the men gave to Gideon. They gave him decorations, necklaces, and purple robes that the kings of Midian had worn.

The men also gave him chains from the camels of the kings of Midian. *Lord, my reward is in Heaven. I know You'll take care of my needs on earth.*

Now Gideon used some of this gold to make an ephod. (Originally, this special chest plate was only to be used by a ruler only as an official insignia, just as David did in First Chronicles 15:27, not for an idolatrous purpose.) He put the ephod in his hometown of Ophrah, but eventually the people of Israel were unfaithful to God and began to worship it as an idol. So Gideon's ephod became a trap that caused Gideon and his family to sin. *Lord, help me to be careful of unintended consequences.*

The Israelites humbled the Midianites so that Midian did not cause any more trouble. And the land had peace from war for 40 years, as long as Gideon was alive.

Gideon ("Jerub-Baal," or "Baal fighter") the son of Joash went to live in his own home. He fathered 70 sons. He had many sons because he had many wives. Gideon had a concubine who lived in Shechem who gave birth to a son. He named that son "Abimelech" (meaning "my father is king"). Gideon, the son of Joash, died at a ripe old age and was buried in the tomb of Joash, his father. That tomb was in Ophrah, where the Abiezrites lived. *Lord, I will remember those who gave me peace.*

As soon as Gideon died, the Israelites became unfaithful to God again. They started following the Baals. They adopted for themselves Baal-Berith as their god. The Israelites did not remember the Lord their God, even though He had saved them from all of their enemies who were living all around them. Now Jerub-Baal, that is Gideon, had done many good things for Israel. However, Israel was not grateful to the family of Gideon for anything. *Lord, teach me gratitude.*

Deception of Abimelech

SCRIPTURE: JUDGES 9

Abimelech, the son of Gideon, went to his uncles who lived in the city
of Shechem. He said to them and to all of his mother's clan,
"Ask all the lords of Shechem this question: 'Is it better for you
to be ruled by the 70 sons of Gideon or to be ruled by only one
man?' Remember, I am your own flesh and blood." Abimelech's
uncles spoke to all the lords of Shechem about him. They asked
them that same question, so the lords decided to follow
Abimelech. They said, "He is related to us." So the lords of
Shechem gave Abimelech about 1¾ pounds of silver from the
temple of the god Baal-Berith. Abimelech used this silver to hire
some worthless, reckless men, who followed Abimelech wherever
he went. *Lord, help me look beyond a person's physical family to
see their spiritual relationships.*

Abimelech went to Ophrah, the hometown of his father, and murdered
his 70 half-brothers. They were the sons of his father, Gideon.
He killed them all on one stone (probably an execution block).
But Gideon's youngest son, Jotham, escaped and hid from
Abimelech. Then all of the lords of Shechem and Beth-Millo
gathered beside the great tree at the stone pillar in Shechem.
There they made Abimelech their king. (All the Canaanite chieftains were called "kings," but that title had not yet been
bestowed by any Jew.)

When Jotham heard about this, he went and stood on the top of Mount
Gerizim (this mountain is so close to Shechem, that the people
could easily hear Jotham's voice). Calling out, Jotham shouted to
the people: "Listen to me, you lords of Shechem, then God may

listen to your prayers. One day, the trees went out to anoint a king to rule over them. They said to the olive tree, 'Become our king!' But the olive tree said to them, 'Men and gods are honored by my oil. Should I stop making olive oil just to go and wave back and forth over the other trees?' Next, the trees said to the fig tree, 'Come, be our king.' But the fig tree answered them, 'Should I quit making my sweet, good fruit merely to go and wave back and forth over the other trees?' Then the trees said to the vine, 'Come, be our king!' But the vine answered them, 'My wine makes men and gods happy. Should I cease making it merely to go and wave back and forth over the other trees?' Finally, all the trees said to the thorn bush, 'Come, be our king.' But the thorn bush said to the trees, 'If you really want to anoint me as king over you, then come and find shelter in my shade. But if you do not want to do this, then let fire come out of the thorn bush to burn up the cedars of Lebanon.

"Now were you completely honest and loyal when you made Abimelech your king? Have you been faithful to Gideon and his family? Have you treated Gideon as you should? Remember, my father Gideon fought for you. He risked his life to save you from the control of the Midianites. But now you have turned against my father's family. You have killed my father's 70 sons on one stone. You have made Abimelech your king over the people of Shechem. And Abimelech is only the son of my father's concubine. You have made Abimelech your king just because he is your relative. So then, if you have been honest and loyal to Gideon and his family today, may you have much happiness with Abimelech as your king. And may he be happy with you people. But if you have not behaved uprightly, may fire come out of Abimelech. May that fire completely burn up you citizens of Shechem and Beth-Millo. That fire will come out of the lords of Shechem and Abimelech himself will burn up." *Lord, Jotham's logic was sound; give me a sound, reasoning mind.*

Then Jotham ran away. He escaped to the city of Beer, and lived there, away from his half-brother Abimelech. So Abimelech ruled over Israel for three years. Then God sent an evil spirit to cause trouble between Abimelech and the lords of Shechem, so that the lords of Shechem turned against Abimelech.

Abimelech had killed the 70 sons of Gideon, who were Abimelech's own half-brothers. And the lords of Shechem had helped him to kill them.

Now, some Shechemite men were attacking and robbing everyone who came by. The lords of Shechem put men on the hilltops to prevent Abimelech from discovering that they were robbing the passing caravans. Nevertheless Abimelech learned about these attacks.

A man named Gaal and his brothers moved into Shechem; Gaal was the son of Ebed. The lords of Shechem decided to trust Gaal and follow him. The people of Shechem went out to the vineyards to pick grapes, walking on top of the grapes to make wine. Then they had a feast in the temple of their god. The people ate and drank and cursed Abimelech. Then Gaal the son of Ebed said, "We are the men of Shechem, why should we obey Abimelech? Who does he think he is? Isn't Abimelech one of Gideon's sons? Didn't Abimelech make Zebul his officer? Should we obey Abimelech? We should not obey the men of Hamor, Shechem's father. Why should we obey Abimelech? If you make me the commander of these people, then I would get rid of Abimelech. I would tell him: 'Get your army ready and come out to do battle.'"

Now Zebul was the governor of Shechem, and he heard what Gaal the son of Ebed said. Zebul became very angry, and sent secret messengers to Abimelech in the city of Arumah, saying, "Gaal the son of Ebed and Gaal's brothers have come to Shechem. Listen, they are turning the city against you. So now, you and your troops should get up in the night. Then go wait in the fields outside the city. When the sun comes up in the morning, get up and attack the city. Listen, Gaal and his men will come out to fight you. Then do whatever you can to them."

So Abimelech—and all of his troops with him—got up during the night. They came near Shechem and separated into four groups. They took up concealed positions near the city. Now Gaal, the son of Ebed, went out and was standing at the entrance to the city gate. Abimelech and his troops jumped up out of their hiding places to attack him. When Gaal saw the soldiers, he said to Zebul, "Look, there are troops coming down from tops of the mountains." But Zebul said, "You are mistaking the shadows of the mountains for men." But again Gaal said, "Look, there are troops coming down from the high ground. And there is one group coming from the tree of the direction of the Diviner's Oak," a well-known landmark in that area. Then Zebul said to Gaal, "Where is your bragging mouth now? You said, 'Who is Abimelech? Why should we obey him?' You made fun of these men. Now, go out and fight them." So Gaal led the men of Shechem out to fight. But Abimelech and his troops chased them. Many of Gaal's men were killed before they could get back to the city gate.

Then Abimelech stayed at Arumah, and Zebul forced Gaal and his brothers to leave Shechem. The next day the people of Shechem went out to the fields. And this was reported to Abimelech. So Abimelech separated his troops into three groups. And he hid them in the fields. When Abimelech saw the people coming out of the city, he jumped up and attacked them. (While the attack was occurring in the fields, another company of soldiers seized the approach to the gates of the city, thereby cutting off their path of retreat.) Abimelech and his group charged forward to the entrance gate of the city. The other two groups charged out to the people in the fields and killed them. (These farm workers were only tending their crops; they did not have their weapons with them.) Abimelech and his men fought against the city of Shechem all that day. They captured it and killed its people. Then Abimelech tore down the whole city, and scattered salt over the ruins so that nothing would ever grow there. (Shechem was devastated about 1150 B.C. Archaeologists from Harvard University have discovered that the nearby temple-fortress was the largest one in all of Palestine.)

The people who lived at the nearby Tower of Shechem heard what had happened to Shechem. So the lords gathered at the stronghold of the temple of the god, Baal-Berith. Abimelech heard that all the lords of the Tower of Shechem had gathered there, so he and all his troops went up to Mount Zalmon near Shechem. Abimelech took an ax and cut off some branches, then put them on his shoulders. He said to his troops who were with him, "Hurry. Do what you have seen me do." So all those men cut down more branches and followed Abimelech. They piled their branches up at the stronghold, then set them on fire and burned up the stronghold. So all the people who lived inside the Tower of Shechem also died. That included about 1,000 men and women.

Then Abimelech went to the city of Thebez (about six miles away), and surrounded the city, attacking it, and capturing it. But inside the city was a strong tower. All the men and women of the lords of that city ran into that tower. When they got inside, they locked the door behind them. Then they climbed up to the roof of the tower. Abimelech came to that tower and attacked it. He went up close to the door of that tower to set it on fire. However, as Abimelech came near, a woman dropped a large stone for grinding grain on top of his head. The stone cracked his skull.

Abimelech quickly called to his young man who carried his armor, "Take out your sword and kill me! I don't want people to say, 'A woman killed Abimelech!'" So the young man ran him through with a sword, and Abimelech died. When the men of Israel saw that Abimelech was dead, they all went back home. So God punished Abimelech for all the evil that he had done. Abimelech had sinned against his own father, Gideon, by murdering Abimelech's 70 half-brothers. God also punished the men of Shechem for the evil they had done. So the curse which Jotham had spoken did come true (see Judg. 9:20). Jotham was a son of Gideon. *Lord, You include the evil done by men in Your book to show us that You use evil to punish evil. I will live righteously.*

Tola

SCRIPTURE: JUDGES 10

After Abimelech died, Tola, the son of Puah, rose up to rescue the people of Israel. Tola was a man from the tribe of Issachar who lived in the city of Shamir in the hill-country of Ephraim. Tola was the leader of Israel for 23 years. Then Tola died, and he was buried in Shamir. *Lord, this unknown man served You; may I do likewise.*

Jair

After Tola died, Jair became the judge of Israel for 22 years. He lived in the region of Gilead. Jair had 30 sons who rode on 30 donkeys. These 30 sons controlled 30 towns in Gilead. These towns are called Havvoth-Jair (the Towns of Jair) to this day. Jair died and was buried in the city of Kamon. *Lord, thank You for men who had faithful sons.*

The Israelites Abandon the Lord Again

Again, the Israelites did evil in the sight of the Lord. They worshiped the Baals and Ashtareth idols. They also worshiped the gods of the peoples of Syria, Sidon, Moab, and Ammon. And, they worshiped the gods of the Philistines. The Israelites abandoned the Lord and stopped serving Him. So the Lord became angry with them. He allowed the Philistines and the Ammonites to defeat them.

In the same year, those people crushed and oppressed the Israelites who lived east of the Jordan River. This is in the region of Gilead, where the Amorites lived. The Israelites suffered for 18 years. The Ammonites also crossed over the Jordan River to fight the people of Judah, Benjamin, and Ephraim. The Ammonites caused much trouble for the people of Israel.

So the Israelites cried out to the Lord, "We have sinned against You. We have abandoned our God and worshiped the Baal idols." The Lord answered the Israelites, "You cried out to Me when the Egyptians, the Amorites, the Ammonites, and the Philistines hurt you. I saved you from those people. You cried to Me when the Sidonians, the Amalekites, and the Maonites oppressed you. I also saved you out of their control. But you have now abandoned Me. You have worshiped different gods. Therefore, I refuse to save you again. You have chosen those gods. So go call on them for help. Let them save you when you get in trouble." But the people of Israel said to the Lord, "We have sinned. Do to us whatever you want, but please save us today." Then the Israelites got rid of the foreign gods among them, and worshiped the Lord again. When He saw their suffering, He felt sorry for them. The Ammonite people gathered for war and camped in Gilead. The Israelites gathered and camped at Mizpah. The leaders of the people of Gilead said to each other, "Who will lead us to attack the people of Ammon? He will become the head of all those who live in Gilead." *Lord, thank You for recognizing real repentance in the past. It means You will recognize my repentance when I cry unto You.*

Jephthah

SCRIPTURE: JUDGES 11

Jephthah was from the people of Gilead. He was a strong warrior. (Jephthah became a man of great faith, see Heb. 11:32.) His father was named Gilead, but his mother was a prostitute. Gilead's wife had several sons for him. When they grew up, they forced Jephthah to leave their home, saying, "You will not inherit any of our fathers' property, because you are the son of another woman" (Jephthah was a half-breed—half-Canaanite and half-Jewish, and an illegitimate son). So Jephthah ran away from his brothers and lived in the land of Tob. There was a group of adventurers who began to follow Jephthah. *Lord, help me remember that sin divides families.*

After a time, the Ammonite people made war against Israel. At that time, the elders of Gilead came to Jephthah asking him to come back from the land of Tob to Gilead, saying, "Come and take command of our army, so we can fight the Ammonites."

But Jephthah said to the elders of Gilead, "Didn't you hate me? You forced me out of my father's house. Why are you coming to me now that you are in trouble?"

The elders of Gilead said to Jephthah, "That is the reason why we are coming to you now. You must come with us and fight against the Ammonites. Then you will be the ruler over everyone who lives in Gilead." Jephthah answered the elders of Gilead, "If you take me back to Gilead to fight the Ammonites, and the Lord gives me victory, then I will become your ruler." The elders of Gilead said to Jephthah, "The Lord is listening to everything we are saying. We promise to do all that you tell us to do." So Jephthah went with the elders of Gilead, and the people made him their ruler and commander of their army. Jephthah repeated all of his words in front of the Lord at Mizpah. (Jephthah probably did not trust them. He was careful to ratify their oath with the general assembly and confirm it in order to make the contract doubly binding.) Jephthah sent messengers to the king of the Ammonites asking the king, "What have you got against Israel? Why have you come to attack our land?" *Lord, it's always wise to negotiate before shedding blood.*

The king of the Ammonites answered the messengers of Jephthah: "We are fighting Israel because you took our land when you came up from Egypt. (This was a false claim.) Israel took our land—from the Arnon River and the Jabbok River, all the way to the Jordan River. Now tell the people of Israel to give our lands back to us in peace." Jephthah sent the messengers of the Ammonite king again, saying, "This is what Jephthah says: 'Israel did not take the land of the people of Moab or the land of Ammon. When the people of Israel came out of Egypt, they went into the desert. They went to the Red Sea and then traveled to Kadesh. Israel sent messengers to the king of Edom, asking, "Please give us permission to go through your country." But the king of Edom would not let us. We sent the same message to the king of Moab. But he would not let us go across his land either. So the Israelites stayed at Kadesh. Next, the Israelites went into the desert. They went around the borders of the lands of Edom and Moab. Israel traveled around the borders of the lands of Edom and Moab. Israel traveled east to the land of Moab. They camped on the other side of the Arnon River. It was the border of the land of Moab. The Israelites did not cross the border to go into the land of Moab.

"'Then Israel sent messengers to Sihon, the king of the Amorites. Sihon
was the king of the city of Heshbon. The messengers of Israel
asked Sihon, "Please let us pass through your land. We want to
go to our country." But Sihon did not trust the Israelites. He
wouldn't let them cross his land. Instead, Sihon gathered all of
his army and camped at Jahaz, and they made war against
Israel. But the Lord, the God of Israel, handed Sihon and all of
Sihon's army over to the Israelites. So Israel struck them down.
And Israel seized all of the land of the Amorites who once lived
there. So Israel seized all of the territory of the Amorites. It
extended from the Arnon River to the Jabbok River, from the
desert to the Jordan River. It was Yahweh, the God of Israel,
who forced out the Amorites ahead of His people of Israel. So
do you think you can force the people of Israel to leave this
land? Surely you can possess the land which your god Chemosh
has given to you [sarcasm]. In the same way, we will possess the
land which the Lord, our God, has dispossessed to give to us.

"'Are you any better than Balak, the son of Zippor? He was the king of
Moab. Did he ever quarrel or fight against the people of Israel?
For 300 years the Israelites have lived in Heshbon and Aroer, as
well as the villages around them. They have lived for 300 years in
all the towns beside the banks of the Arnon River. Why have you
not taken those towns back during all that time? Therefore, I have
not sinned against you! But you are sinning against me by declar-
ing war on me. May the Lord, the Judge, decide today whether the
Israelites or the Ammonites are right.'" But the king of the
Ammonites ignored this message which Jephthah sent to him.
Lord, Jephthah's logic was right, the false gods have no power.

Jephthah's Vow

Then the Spirit of the Lord came upon Jephthah. Jephthah passed
through Gilead and Manasseh, coming to the city of Mizpah in
Gilead. From there, Jephthah passed through to the land of the
Ammonites. Jephthah made a vow to the Lord saying, "If You, O
God, will truly give me victory over the Ammonites, then I will
give you a whole burnt offering (something that was being
offered to God completely). I will sacrifice the first thing that
comes out of my house to meet me when I return after the victory.
It will belong to the Lord." Then Jephthah went over to fight
against the Ammonites. And the Lord gave Jephthah the victory
over the Ammonites. Jephthah struck them down from the city
of Aroer to the area of Minnith. He defeated them as far as the
city of Abel-Keramim. He defeated 20 towns in this region, and
the destruction was tremendous. So the Ammonites were humbled by the Israelites. When Jephthah returned home to Mizpah,
his own daughter came out to meet him. She was playing a tam-
bourine and dancing. She was Jephthah's only child; he did not
have any other sons or daughters. *Lord, You include these difficult passages in Scripture because they reflect the difficult decisions Your servants had to make.*

When Jephthah saw his daughter, he tore his clothes and said, "O no,
my daughter. You have made me sad. (Jephthah knew that he
would never have descendents, because she was his only daughter. So it was the end of his posterity upon the earth.) This is
because I have made a vow to the Lord, and I cannot break it."
Then his daughter said to him, "O father, you made a vow to the
Lord. So do to me just what you vowed, because the Lord gave
you the victory over your enemies, the Ammonites." Then she
said to her father, "But let me do this one thing first. Let me be
alone for two months; let me go down into the hill-country. I
will never marry. So let me and my girlfriends go and cry together."

Jephthah said, "Go." And he sent her away for two months. She and her girlfriends went to the hill-country, and there they wept for her because she would never marry. After two months, she returned to her father, and he did to her what he vowed to the Lord. (Since Jephthah was a man who had the Spirit of God within him [see Judg. 11:29], and Jephthah was thoroughly familiar with the Law of Moses, Jephthah knew that human sacrifice was wrong [see Gen. 22:1-19; Lev. 18:21; 20:2; Deut. 12:31. Compare Second Kings 3:27; 16:3; 23:10; Second Chron. 28:3; Mic. 6:6-8; Jer. 19:5]. The Torah stated that the firstborn were the "redeemed." We believe that Jephthah's daughter was solemnly dedicated to God's service at the Tabernacle in Shiloh for the rest of her life. Compare the actions of Hannah in First Samuel 1:11 with regard to young Samuel.) Jephthah's daughter never had a husband. *Lord, teach me the power of vows.*

So this had become a custom in Israel: Every year, the women of Israel go out to God's Tabernacle at Shiloh, where Jephthah's daughter was for four days. They do this to tell the story of the daughter of Jephthah who came from Gilead.

The Story of Inappropriate Jephthah

Judges 11

Date: 1161 B.C. ↗ Place: Gilead

If ever there was an "inappropriate" leader, it sure was Jephthah. He was the son of perhaps the most prominent leader in Gilead, because his father was named Gilead, and we don't know if the city was named for the father, or the father named after the city. But Jephthah was the child of a harlot, one that carries a certain social stigma in most societies. *Lord, remind me that social standing doesn't guarantee spiritual standing.*

But Jephthah's mother was just a "used" prostitute; I'm sure prominent Jewish men visited "inappropriate" Jewish prostitutes. Both would have known they were breaking God's seventh commandment. *Lord, thank You for mercy out of sin.*

Jephthah's mother was a Canaanite, making him half-Jewish and half-Canaanite, or in reality a half-breed. Maybe his background gave him a "wild" nature. He didn't accept the status of his half-brothers or his father. His half-brothers ran him out of the house and refused to share his father's inheritance with him. *Lord, I'm glad for this rebel that You used greatly.*

Jephthah left the Promised Land and home of his father to live in Tob, half way to Damascus of Syria; in the wilderness. He must have been an authentic leader; about 400 "outcasts" joined him in "no-man's-land." They ran a "protection agency," much like the Mob or terrorists in some places. They protected farmers and shop keepers from rogues and desert nomadic raiders for a "price." The farmers gave Jephthah and his men part of what they raised for "protection." *Lord, I'm glad You love and use unusual people.*

When the nation of Ammon was ready to attack Gilead and the surrounding areas, the leaders of Gilead realize they didn't have a military leader, so they negotiated with Jephthah. Since he negotiated payment with farmers in Tob, he did the same with Gilead. Jephthah told them he'd lead them into war and win it, but afterward, he wanted to be the "political" leader of Gilead. He wanted respectability. To make sure the leaders of Gilead would keep their part of the bargain, they went to the Tabernacle, and Jephthah made them agree to his conditions before God. *Lord, a well-negotiated contract makes good friends and working relationships.*

Next, Jephthah negotiated with Ammon. He wanted to find out why Gilead was being attacked. The problem back then is the same land problem in modern Israel, "Who originally owned the land?" Ammon claimed they were living there when Joshua and the Jews out of Egypt took it from them. Don't modern-day Palestinians claim modern-day Israel has taken their land, but did not David and the kings of Israel own it in Old Testament times? Didn't God promise the land originally to Abraham? *Lord it's Your land; it doesn't belong to any nation, and Jesus will live there during the Millennium.*

Jephthah told Ammon that his God—Jehovah—had delivered the land to Israel in war. Then Jephthah got sarcastic, "If your god Molech is a true god, why didn't he protect it for you?"

The Spirit of God came on Jephthah, and he led his army out to battle. From what we know about the Spirit's filling, Jephthah must have yielded to God, and earnestly prayed for the Spirit's anointing. *Lord, fill me for service just as You did Jephthah.*

Jephthah was a spiritual man of faith according to Hebrews 11:32. He vowed that if God would give him victory, when he got back home he'd sacrifice the first thing that came out of his house to meet him. God gave him the victory. When he got home, the first thing to meet him was his daughter. Jephthah was overwhelmed because he'd have to keep his word to God. *Lord, I'll keep my promises just as Jephthah.*

Some of the old commentaries teach Jephthah sacrificed his daughter as a whole burnt offering. Maybe it's the King James phrase that makes them think that. But that view is against all of the teaching of Scripture.

First, God prohibited child sacrifice, and that was one of the worst sins of Ammon. Jephthah couldn't sacrifice his daughter and be a Spirit-filled member of God's Hall of Faith (see Heb. 11). Second, Jephthah made his vow when he was Spirit filled. In the third place, why was Jephthah so grief stricken when he saw his daughter come running out of the house to meet him? Jephthah knew she would be dedicated to God, probably in a Tabernacle service, just as young Samuel. That meant Jephthah would have no heir to carry on his name and inheritance. She would be a virgin for life. Reputation was important to Jephthah who grew up without a respectable reputation. No wonder he was grief stricken. *Lord, may I look beyond physical reputation to an inheritance with You.*

My Time to Pray

Lord, You're not as concerned with our physical birth
  As You are with our spiritual birth;
  Thank You that I've been born again.

Lord, You're not as concerned about our past
  As You are about our future;
  I dedicate my future to You.

Lord, You make me what I am today;
  I will use all I have for Your glory.

  Amen.

Jephthah Defeats Ephraim

SCRIPTURE: JUDGES 12

The men of Ephraim called out all of their soldiers. Then they crossed the Jordan River to the town of Zaphon and said to Jephthah, "Why didn't you cross over to invite us to help you to fight the Ammonites? We will burn your house down—with you in it."

Jephthah answered them, "My people and I have fought a great battle against the Ammonites. I did call you, but you did not come to help me against them. And when I saw that you would not help me, I risked my own life. I went over to fight against the Ammonites, and the Lord gave me victory over them. Now, why have you come to fight against me today?" *Lord, it's so easy for believers to get bitter with one another, then to argue and fight. Help me be understanding of others.*

Then Jephthah gathered all the men of Gilead together and fought against the men of Ephraim. The men of Gilead struck down the Ephraimites because the Ephraimites had insulted them. They had said, "You men of Gilead are nothing but deserters from Ephraim and Manasseh." The men of Gilead captured the crossing places of the Jordan River, those places that led to the country of Ephraim. Sometimes a man from Ephraim trying to escape would say: "Let me cross the river." Then the men of Gilead would ask him: "Are you from Ephraim?" If he said, "No," then they would tell him, "Say the word, 'Shibboleth.'" The men of Ephraim could not pronounce that word correctly ("Shibboleth" means "stream"). If the man from Ephraim said, "Sibboleth," (Sibboleth means "a burden") then the men of Gilead would seize him and kill him at the crossing place of the Jordan River.

So, 42,000 men from Ephraim were killed at that time (as they tried to escape home). Jephthah was a judge for the people of Israel for six years. Then Jephthah from Gilead died. He was buried among the towns in Gilead. *Lord, teach me that arguing and fighting may lead to bloodshed. May I be a person of peace.*

Ibzan

After Jephthah died, Ibzan was a judge for Israel. He was from Bethlehem. He had 30 sons and 30 daughters and permitted his daughters to marry men who were not in his clan. And he brought 30 women who were not in his tribe to be wives for his sons. Ibzan was a leader of Israel for seven years. Then Ibzan died, and he was buried in Bethlehem.

Elon

After Ibzan died, Elon was a judge for Israel. He was from the tribe of Zebulun. He was the judge of Israel for ten years. Then Elon, the man of Zebulun, died. He was buried in the city of Aijalon in the territory of Zebulun.

Abdon

After Elon died, Abdon was a judge for Israel. He was the son of Hillel, the Pirathonite. He had 40 sons and 30 grandsons, who rode 70 donkeys. He led Israel for eight years. Then Abdon, the son of Hillel, died. He was buried in Pirathon, in the territory of Ephraim, in the hill-country of the Amalekites. *Lord, nothing is said about the accomplishments of Ibzan, Elon, and Abdon, except they faithfully did their task as judges. If I accomplish nothing in life, may I be found faithful.*

Samson's Birth

SCRIPTURE: JUDGES 13

Again the people of Israel did what was evil in the sight of the Lord. So
God handed them over to the Philistines for 40 years. There was
a man named Manoah from the town of Zorah. Manoah was
from the tribe of Dan. He had a wife, but she could not have
children. The Angel of the Lord appeared to Manoah's wife, and
said, "You have not been able to have children, but you will now
become pregnant and have a son. Be sure that you don't drink
any wine or strong drink. And don't eat anything that is
unclean. You will become pregnant and give birth to a son. You
must never cut his hair, because he will be a Nazirite. From
birth, he will be devoted to God, and will begin the work of sav-
ing Israel from the control of the Philistines." *Lord, thank You for
godly mothers who raise up their children to serve You.*

Then Manoah's wife went to her husband and told him what had happened, telling him, "A Man from God came to me. He looked
like an angel from the one true God. His appearance was so
awesome that I didn't ask him where he was from. And he didn't
tell me his name. But he told me, 'You will become pregnant,
and will give birth to a son. Don't drink any wine or strong
drink, and don't eat anything that is unclean, because the boy
will be a Nazirite (a Nazirite made a vow to the Lord which was
usually a temporary self-imposed discipline of abstaining from
wine, unshaven hair, not touching dead bodies and/or unclean
food—some "Nazirites for life" found in the Bible were: Samson
[Judg. 13:7; 16:17], Samuel [1 Sam. 1:11], and John the
Immerser.) He will be a Nazirite from his birth until the day he

dies.'" *Lord, may I follow You as carefully as the Nazirites mentioned in Scripture.*

Then Manoah prayed to the Lord: "O my Lord, please let the Man of God whom You sent, come to us again. Let him teach us what we should do for the boy who will be born to us." *Lord, thank You for the prayers of godly mothers.*

God listened to Manoah's prayer. The Angel of God did come to Manoah's wife again as she was sitting in a field, but her husband was not with her. So she quickly ran to tell her husband, saying, "He is here. The Man who appeared to me the other day is here." Manoah got up and followed his wife. When he got to the Man, Manoah said, "Are you the Man who spoke to my wife?" The Man said, "I am." So Manoah asked, "Now, when your words come true, what kind of life should the boy live? And, what will he do?" The Angel of the Lord said to Manoah, "Your wife must be very careful to do everything I told her to do. She must not eat anything that grows on a grapevine. She must not drink any wine or strong drink. She must not eat anything that is unclean. She must be very careful to do everything I have commanded her." *Lord, I will abstain from alcohol, unclean activities, and unwholesome things.*

Manoah said to the Angel of the Lord, "We would like you to stay for awhile. Please, let us prepare a young goat in Your presence (a whole burnt offering) to worship." The Angel of the Lord answered Manoah, "Even though I will stay awhile, I will not eat your food. But, if you prepare something, offer a whole burnt offering to Yahweh." Manoah did not yet realize that the Man was really the Angel of the Lord. Then Manoah asked the Angel of the Lord, "What is your name? That we may honor You when Your words come true." The Angel of the Lord said, "Why do you ask My name? It is Wonderful (see Isa. 9:6)." *Lord Jesus, Your name is Wonderful because of Your character and accom-*

plishments. I worship You with the sacrifice of my life to serve You.

Then Manoah took a young goat and sacrificed it upon a rock. He also offered a food offering to the Lord. Then the Angel of the Lord did an amazing thing; Manoah and his wife were watching when it happened. The flames went up to the sky from the altar. As the fire was burning, the Angel of the Lord went up to Heaven in the fire of the altar. When Manoah and his wife saw that, they bowed facedown on the ground. The Angel of the Lord never appeared to Manoah or to his wife again. Then Manoah realized that the Man really *was* the Angel of the Lord. Manoah said to his wife, "We have seen *God!* We will surely die." But his wife said to him, "The Lord does not want to kill us. If He did, He would not have accepted our whole burnt offering and the food offering from our hands. And He would not have revealed all of these things to us. And he would not have caused us to hear such things as these." *Lord, thank You for the leadership of faithful fathers.*

So the woman gave birth to a son, and she named him "Samson." (The Hebrew name means "little sun" or "sunny.") Samson grew up, and the Lord blessed him. The Spirit of the Lord began to work in Samson. This was while he was in the city of Mahaneh-Dan. It is between the cities of Zorah and Eshtaol. *Lord, thank You for the Holy Spirit that works in young children to prepare them for Your service.*

Judges 13

The Story Behind Manoah's Good Wife

And Manoah said unto his wife, "We shall surely die, because we have seen God." But his wife said to him, "If the Lord were pleased to kill us, He would not have received a burnt offering and a meat offering at our hands, neither would He have showed us all these things, nor would as at this time have told us such things as these" (Judges 13:22-23).

Have you ever prayed for something that made you tremble with fear? Manoah asked to see the Angel of the Lord that his wife had seen, and then when Manoah saw the Lord, he thought he was going to die. The One called Wonderful—the Lord Jesus Christ for this was a Christophany—appeared to him. When Manoah saw the Wonderful One he cried, "We have seen God, we shall surely die." When you pray for something and God's answer scares you almost to death, look by faith to God. Charles Spurgeon says, "The blessings we so eagerly implore...is the occasion of suffering which we deplore."[1] *Lord, sometimes I grumble when things go wrong, yet You are answering my prayer. Forgive me!*

Look at the faith of Manoah and his wife. When she told her husband about the Angel of the Lord she saw, and His promise of a male child, he believed God. When Manoah prayed for the Angel for the Lord to return, it was so he would know how to teach the promised son. Was Manoah's faith great or small? Just as you cannot judge a man by one sentence out of his mouth, so Manoah's faith-statement later is countered when he claims he'll die. *Lord, give me constant faith to always say the right thing.*

Next look at the faith of the wife. She was the "weaker vessel," but the stronger believer. Let's ask an innocent question, "Why did the Angel of the Lord appear to her first and not the husband?" Maybe angels go first to those who have the strongest faith. And maybe angels desire to speak to those who will receive their message from God. Does not Hebrews tell us that angels are "sent forth to minister to them who shall be heirs of salvation" (Heb. 1:14)? *Lord, if I've ever seen an angel, I don't know it, but I believe they are Your messengers.*

Some say a woman is all heart, they can't reason, nor do they tend to be logical. Yet, here is Manoah's wife with more logic than her husband. While he's expressing the emotions of fear, she uses logic to calm the fears of both of them. *Lord, I believe women can do much more than most men think they can do.*

Notice the three things that the wife argues that reflects her great faith. First, she argues the Wonderful One did not intend to kill them because He accepted their sacrifices. The next time your doubts scare you to death, and you think you'll die because you've displeased the Lord, remember the Father has accepted the sacrifice of His Son on Calvary in place of your sin. You won't die—perhaps, now you'll live forever. The heavenly Father accepts you as perfect in His Son—justified—as if you've never sinned. *Lord, I stand in Christ; that's the only standing room I've got.*

The second wise thing the wife said, "Neither would He have showed us all these things." What's more wonderful to an infertile woman than the news she's going to get pregnant and have a child? Also, she heard that her son was going to begin delivering her people from the Philistines. This was better than good news, this was great news—no, it was Wonderful. *Lord, my deliverance from sin is Wonderful news.*

The third logic of Manoah's wife was pragmatic appeal, "Nor would He at this time have told us such things as these." Manoah prayed for the Angel to reappear, and He did. Then he was afraid of dying (we shouldn't be afraid of God's answer to our prayers). The couple got precious promises. Think of God's Old Testament promises to send a Savior—they were all fulfilled. Think of God's Bible promises to save you—they were all fulfilled. Think of God's promise to hear your prayers. What say you? "This poor man cried and the Lord heard him and delivered him from all his fears." If you have proved in the past the faithfulness of God to answer your prayers, then trust Him today. *Lord, when I look in the rear view mirror, I have greater faith.*

Praise God for Manoah whose prayer was answered. Praise God for the logical assurance from the wife's faith. *Lord, I believe.*

Endnote

1. Metropolitan Tabernacle Pulpit, "Manoah's Wife and Her Excellent Arguement," sermons preached and revised 1877, 110, <http://books .google.com/books?id=ZH8PAAAAIAAJ&pg=PA110&lpg=PA110&dq= sPURGEON+SERMON+bLESSINGS+WE+SO+EAGERLY+IMPLORE& source=bl&ots=CdjpmEMfz8&sig=2L9ibupJMxUZywIlIOiRUNCRpAU& hl=en&ei=8XCtSdusIovltgfLlZ2LBg&sa=X&oi=book_result&resnum=1&ct =result#PPA109,M1,> (accessed 3 March 2009).

Samson's First Wife

SCRIPTURE: JUDGES 14

Samson went down to the town of Timnah. There he saw one of the daughters of the Philistines. When Samson returned home, he told his father and his mother: "I have seen one of the daughters of the Philistines down in Timnah. I want you to get her for me now as a wife." (According to Deuteronomy 7:3-4, such a marriage was forbidden.) His father and mother answered, "Surely there is a woman from Israel that you can marry. Why the Philistines? The Philistines are not even circumcised." (They were not in a covenant relationship with Yahweh.) But Samson said to his father, "No! Get that girl for me. She is the one I want!" (The father was the person to arrange to pay a formal dowry-price to the prospective bride's family.) Samson's parents did not know that the Lord was involved. God was looking for a way to confront the Philistines, because they were ruling over Israel at that time. *Lord, I pray that young people may marry "in the Lord" and serve You through their marriage.*

Samson went down with this father and his mother to Timnah to arrange the marriage. Later, a young lion came suddenly toward Samson in the vineyards of Timnah (Samson should not have been near the fruit of the vine) roaring as it came. The Spirit of the Lord entered Samson with great power. Samson tore the young lion apart with his bare hands. For Samson, it was as easy as tearing apart a young goat. But Samson did not tell his father or his mother what he had done. Then Samson went down to Timnah to talk to the Philistine girl that he liked. *Lord,*

it's easy to compromise my separation from the world when I
view life through my desires and not through Your will.

Several days later, Samson went back to marry her. On his way, he went over to look at the body of the dead lion. He found a swarm of bees in it, and they had made some honey there. Samson got some of the honey with his hands and walked along, eating it. When he came to his parents, he gave some to them. They ate it, too. But Samson did not tell them that he had taken the honey from the body of the dead lion. (As a Nazirite, it was forbidden for Samson to touch a dead thing [see Num. 6:6]. If his parents had known that fact, they would not have eaten this honey.) Samson's father went down to meet the Philistine girl. The custom was for the groom to give a feast. So Samson gave a banquet. When the Philistines saw Samson, they sent 30 men to be with Samson (friends of the groom). Then Samson said to the 30 men, "Let me tell you a riddle. This wedding feast will last for seven days. Try to guess the answer during that time. If you can, then I will give you 30 linen shirts. I will also give you 30 sets of clothes (outer garments made of wool). However, if you cannot tell me the answer, then you must pay me. You must give me 30 linen shirts and 30 sets of clothes." So they said to Samson, "Tell us your riddle. We will listen to it." Samson said to the Philistine men, "Out of the eater comes something to eat. Out of the strong comes forth something sweet."

The 30 men tried for three days to figure it out, but they could not find the answer. On the fourth day, they went to Samson's fiancée and said, "Did you invite us here to embarrass us? Persuade your husband-to-be into telling us the answer to the riddle. If you don't, we will burn you up—and everyone else in your father's household." *Lord, satan knew the weakness of Samson—women. May satan not get to me through my weakness.*

So Samson's fiancée went to him and began to cry, saying, "You hate me. You don't really love me. You told the riddle to my people, but you won't tell me the answer."

But Samson said to her, "I haven't even told my father or my mother. Why should I tell you?"

Samson's fiancée wept for the rest of the seven days of the feast. So Samson finally gave her the answer on the seventh day. Then she revealed the answer to the riddle to her own people. The Philistine men of the town said to Samson: "What is sweeter than honey? What is stronger than a lion?"

Then Samson said to them, "If you had not plowed with my little heifer, you would not have solved my riddle."

The Spirit of the Lord entered Samson in a powerful way. Samson went down to the city of Ashkelon (about 24 miles west-by-southwest from Timnah). He killed 30 Philistine men and took all their belongings (plunder). He gave those sets of clothes to the men who had guessed the riddle. Then Samson went to his father's house very angry. Now Samson's fiancée was given away to Samson's "best man" to become his wife. *Lord, outward anger comes from lack of inward self-control. This is a strange mixture of outward "righteous indignation" and fleshly desires. Just as You used Samson who was not perfect, use me; I am not perfect.*

More Women Problems

SCRIPTURE: JUDGES 15

Later, at the time of the wheat harvest, Samson went to visit his fiancée. He took a young goat with him. (Since the fiancée still lived in her father's house, it was customary to carry some gift. It was Samson's token of reconciliation.) He thought: "I'm going to have sex with my wife." But, her father would not allow Samson to enter the house. Her father said, "I thought you really hated your fiancée. So I gave her to your 'best man' when you left the wedding. Her younger sister is more beautiful. Take her instead." *Lord, teach me when I compromise my Christian standards, I get unsought consequences.*

But Samson said, "Now I have cause to harm you Philistines. This time, no one will blame me." So Samson went out and caught 300 jackals ("foxes"). He took two jackals at a time and tied their tails together. Then he put one torch between the tails of each pair of jackals and lit the torches. Then he turned the jackals loose in the standing grain fields of the Philistines. In this way, he burned up their standing grain and the bundles of grain. He also burned up their vineyards and their olive trees. *Lord, keep me from being controlled by revenge.*

The Philistines asked, "Who did this?" Someone told them, "Samson did it, because his father-in-law gave Samson's fiancée to his 'best man.'" So the Philistines went and burned Samson's fiancée and her father to death. *Lord, remind me that my violent temper will lead to my hardship and terrible consequences in the lives of others.*

Then Samson said to the Philistines, "Since you acted like this, I will surely take vengeance on all of you. I won't stop until I pay you back." Samson attacked the Philistines ("and he struck them hip on thigh," a Hebrew proverbial idiom which meant merciless slaughter) and killed many of them. Then he went down and lived in a cave. (A natural fortress in which to hide.) It was in the Rock of Etam (two miles southwest of Bethlehem). This spot is a sheer, vertical cliff with a large cave, which is very difficult to access.) *Lord, teach me the principle that a solitary individual with limited resources can be influential for You against the crowd, when that individual is filled with the Spirit of God.*

Samson Kills 1,000 Philistines

Then the Philistines went up and camped in the territory of Judah. They spread out near a place named Lehi. The men of Judah asked, "Why have you come up here, to fight us?"

They answered, "We have come to take Samson as our prisoner. We want to pay him back for what he did to our people."

Then 3,000 men of Judah went down to the cave in the Rock of Etam. They said to Samson, "What have you done to us? Don't you realize that the Philistines rule over us?" *Lord, remind me that when I take a stand for You, many compromising believers will not stand with me, and they may even turn against me.*

Samson answered, "I only paid them back for what they did to me."

Then they said to Samson, "We have come down to tie you up and hand you over to the Philistines."

Samson said, "Promise me that you will not hurt me."

The men from Judah said to him, "We agree. We will merely tie you up and hand you over to the Philistines. We will certainly not kill you." So they tied up Samson with two new ropes, then led him up from the Rock of Etam.

When Samson came to the place named Lehi, the Philistines met him. They were shouting for joy. Then the Spirit of the Lord entered Samson in a powerful way. The ropes on his arms became weak like strings that had been burned. His bonds fell off his wrists. Samson found the jawbone of a donkey that had just died. He seized it and killed 1,000 men with it.

Then Samson said, "With a donkey's jawbone, I have piled them up high." (There is a clever wordplay going on in this verse. Moffatt's translation has: "With the jawbone of an *ass*, I have piled them in a *mass*.") "With a donkey's jawbone, I have killed 1,000 men." When Samson finished speaking, he tossed the jawbone away. So that place was named Ramath-Lehi (the hill of the jawbone). *Lord, remind me that You use ordinary little tools to get Your work done, tools like the jawbone of an ass.*

Samson was very thirsty, so he cried out to the Lord, "I am Your servant. You gave me this great victory. Do I now have to die of thirst? Do I have to be captured by people who are not circumcised?" Then God opened up a hollow place in the ground at Lehi, and water came out. When Samson drank that water, his spirit returned. So that spring was named "En-Hakkore" (the Spring of the Caller). It is still there in Lehi to this day. So Samson led Israel for 20 years. (Samson single-handedly kept the flame of patriotism alive during the long Philistine reign of oppression.) *Lord, remind me that You can use believers who are not prefect. Use me.*

Samson at Gaza

SCRIPTURE: JUDGES 16

Samson went to Gaza. (Gaza was one of the five main Philistine cities.) He saw a prostitute there. He had sex with her. Someone told the people of Gaza: "Samson has come here." So they surrounded the place and hid themselves the entire night to trap him. They waited for him all night at the city gate. They said to each other, "At dawn, we will kill Samson."

But Samson only laid down with the prostitute until midnight. Then he got up and took hold of the doors and the two side-posts of the city gate. He tore them loose, along with the bar. Then he put them on his shoulders and carried them to the top of the hill that faces the city of Hebron (the text is not clear whether Samson took them to the top of the hill that faces Hebron, or he took them 40 miles to Hebron).

Samson and Delilah

After this, Samson fell in love with a woman named Delilah. She lived in the valley of Sorek. The lord of the Philistines went to Delilah, and said, "Try to find out what makes Samson so strong. Try to entice him. Then we will be able to humble him. If you do this, each one of us will pay you 28 pounds of silver." *Lord, teach me to look to You, because some who are close to me will try to destroy me.*

So Delilah said to Samson, "Please tell me why you are so strong. How can someone tie you up and take control of you?"

Samson answered her, "If they tied me up using seven fresh bow-strings which have not been dried, then I would be as weak as any other man."

Then the lord of the Philistines brought seven new bow-strings to Delilah. They had not been dried. And she used them to tie up Samson. Some Philistine men were hiding in an interior room. Delilah said to Samson, "Samson, the Philistines are about to capture you." But Samson easily broke the bow-strings. So the Philistines did not find the secret of Samson's strength. *Lord, remove my blindness about "false friends" who will try to destroy me.*

Then (enough time had passed for Delilah to avoid suspicion) Delilah said to Samson, "Look, you have made a fool out of me. You lied to me. Now please tell me, what could be used to bind you?"

Samson said to her, "To bind me, they would have to use new ropes that have never been used for work. Then I would become as weak as any other man."

So Delilah got some new ropes and tied up Samson with them. Some Philistine men were hiding in a room inside. Then Delilah called out to him, "Samson, the Philistines are about to capture you." But Samson broke the ropes from his arms as if they were threads.

Then Delilah said to Samson, "Now you have mocked me. You have lied to me. Tell me what to use to bind you."

Samson said to her, "Use the loom (a device to make cloth). Weave the seven braids of my head into the loom. Tighten it with a pin. Then I would become as weak as any other man." *Lord, teach me to trust only You, and not trust those who have deceived me in the past.*

Then Samson went to sleep (he was drunk or had been drugged by
Delilah). So Delilah wove the seven braids of his head into the
loom. Then she fastened it with a pin (to keep it firm and
immovable).

Again she called out to him, "Samson, the Philistines are about to capture you." Samson woke up and ripped off the pin and the loom.

Then Delilah said to Samson, "How can you say, 'I love you' when you
won't confide in me? This is the third time that you have made a
fool out of me. You have not told me the secret of your great
strength." Delilah kept on nagging Samson about his secret, day
after day. He became so tired of it that he felt he was going to
die. *Lord, teach me the principle of separation, to avoid those
who have deceived me in the past.*

So Samson told her his whole heart. He said to her, "I have never had
my hair cut. I have been set apart for God as a Nazirite
(Samson's strength did not come from his hair, but from his
relationship to God as a Nazirite) since I was born. If someone
shaved my head, then I would lose my strength. And I would
become as weak as any other man."

Delilah could see that Samson had told her everything sincerely. So she
sent a message to the lords of the Philistines, saying, "Come one
more time, because Samson has told me everything." So the
lords of the Philistines came back to Delilah and brought the
money in their hands. Delilah caused Samson to go to sleep; he
was lying in her lap. Then she called in a Philistine man to shave
off the seven braids of Samson's head. In this way, she made
him weak. So Samson's strength left him. *Lord, I will not share
spiritual secrets with those who don't know You.*

Then she called out to him, "Samson, the Philistines are about to capture you." He woke up and thought: "I'll break loose as I did

231

before and shake myself free." But Samson did *not* know that the Lord had left him. *Lord, never leave me.*

Then the Philistines captured Samson. They gouged out his eyes, and brought him down to Gaza. They bound him with bronze chains and put him in prison and made him grind grain like an ox. But Samson's hair began to grow again. (Samson seems to have reflected on his spiritual blunder, and he seems to have penitently renewed his Nazirite vow.)

Samson's Death

The lord of the Philistines gathered to celebrate and offer a great sacrifice to their god, Dagon. They bragged, "Our god has given Samson, our enemy, into our hands." When the Philistine people saw him, they praised their god, saying, "This man destroyed our country. He killed many of us. But our god has put our enemy into our hands." The people were having such a good time at the celebration that they said, "Bring Samson out to entertain us." So they brought Samson out of the prison. He was a spectacle for them. They made him stand between the pillars of the temple of Dagon. A servant boy was holding his hand. Samson said to him, "Let me feel the pillars that hold up the temple. I want to lean against them." Now the temple was full of men and women. All the lords of the Philistines were there. There were about 3,000 men and women on the roof watching Samson being displayed. *Lord, thank You for Samson's repentance and rededication.*

Then Samson prayed to the Lord saying, "O Lord my Lord, remember me. You are the one true God. Please give me strength one more time. Let me pay these Philistines back for putting out both of my eyes." Then Samson held onto the two pillars in the middle of the temple. These two columns supported the whole temple.

Samson leaned his weight on the two pillars, his right hand on one column, and his left hand on the other column. Samson said, "Let me die with these Philistines" (Samson was praying for an honorable way out of the terrible disgrace that he had brought upon himself and his people). Then he pushed as hard as he could. The temple came down upon the Philistine lords and all the people inside. So Samson killed more Philistines when he died than while he was alive. *Lord, thank You for completing Your intended purpose.*

Samson's brothers and his whole family went down to get his corpse. They carried him back and buried him in the tomb of Manoah, his father. That tomb is between the towns of Zorah and Eshtaol. Samson was a judge for the people of Israel for 20 years. *Lord, I think for what Samson could have done if he completely separated himself to You. I thank You for all he accomplished in spite of his lack of separation from sin.*

Judges 16

The Story About How Samson Lost God's Presence

Date: 1140 B.C. ⌒ Place: Valley of Sorek

And she said, "The Philistines are upon you, Samson!" So he awoke from his sleep, and said, "I will go out as before, at other times, and shake myself free!" But he did not know that the Lord had departed from him (Judges 16:20).

We wrongly think our lives will continue when we do nothing to maintain them. That's because we do not understand *entropy.* The body dies without food, gardens go to weeds if you don't tend it, and a car needs gas and repairs to keep going. The Second Law of

Thermodynamics says all bodies will slow down and eventually stop. Your spiritual life will deteriorate if you don't stay close to the Lord. *Lord, I want to squeeze in close to You.*

Samson had everything going for him. He was born to godly parents who prayed for his birth. The Spirit of the Lord came upon him several times (see Judg. 14:6,19; 15:14) and he was victorious over the Philistines several times. What caused his downfall? Perhaps some of the things that ultimately destroyed Samson's life will plague your walk with God. We'll look at the problem of sin that grew unnoticed. We'll see the ultimate sin that destroyed him. Perhaps this lesson will help you avoid the things that doomed Samson. *Lord, protect me from unobserved dangers.*

Before Samson was born, God promised to use him to defeat the Philistines (see Judg. 13:5), but Samson had a woman problem. First, he fell in love with a Philistine woman and told his parents to arrange a marriage with her. They objected, "Is there no woman among the daughters of your brethren" (Judg. 14:3)? But Samson was hardheaded, "She pleases me well" (Judg. 14:3). Samson chose by the eye of the flesh, he compromised his faith and eventually destroyed the woman and her family. Are you making decisions to satisfy the flesh, decisions that are contrary to God's will for your life? *Lord, I surrender all.*

Next, Samson visited a prostitute in Hebron. Breaking the seventh commandment is bad enough—"You shall not commit adultery"—but Samson visited the town of his enemies to fulfill his lust. The town's people found out Samson was in Hebron and plotted to kill him. Now look at Samson the alleged man of God. He breaks God's law openly, he compromised God's testimony among the heathen, and he opened himself to danger. How can God's servant be so reckless? Have you ever broken God's law and embarrassed the Lord in front of unsaved people? Has your sin ever threatened your physical life? *Lord, keep me in the days of my stupidity.*

Samson escaped the assassination team by using his strength to break down the gate to the city. He escaped carrying off the gate. Shouldn't this brush with death have warned Samson? How many times will God have to deliver you before you learn your lesson about compromise? *Lord, teach me to be careful in all things.*

Samson is best known for the temptation by Delilah. It was a set-up. The rulers of five different Philistine cities promised Delilah money if she would deliver Samson into their hands. The fact they paid a woman of Delilah's reputation tells us Samson did not have a testimony among his enemies. As a matter of fact, they knew his weakness better than he did. *Lord, open my blind eyes to my weaknesses.*

Who knows your weakness? Surely satan knows your vulnerable spots. You should want to be so strong in the Lord that you have no inconsistencies or weak spots in your walk with Christ. And above all, you wouldn't want others to laugh at your sin behind your back. *Lord, help me be strong in every area of my life.*

It took three times for Delilah to learn the secret of Samson's strength. First, Samson told her that if he were bound with seven green vines, he would be as weak as any other man. Delilah tied him with green vines while he was asleep. But he broke them easily when awakened. Second, Samson told her if he were tied with new rope that was never used, he couldn't break them. Again Delilah tied him, but Samson broke them easily. Third, Samson told her if his hair were woven into a loom, he would be weak. Again Samson broke the weavers loom when awakened. Finally, because of her tears, Samson told her that his hair was the symbol of his strength. If she would cut his hair, he would be powerless. *Lord, may I never surrender to the enemy.*

Samson should have immediately left Delilah when she betrayed him the first time. Or at least he should have doubted her and not opened up to her the second and third time. But remember, Samson had a woman problem, and sexual danger seemed to tantalize him. Why are some Christians like Samson; they want to see how close to the edge they could walk, rather than fleeing evil (see 1 Tim. 6:11)? Is that you? What will you have to learn to stay in the middle of the road? *Lord, keep me close to You.*

Each time Samson deceived Delilah about what made him strong, the enemy rushed in to capture him. Samson told a lie; Delilah topped his deception with her deception. It was a dangerous game those lovers played. She, for lust of money, he for lust of the flesh. Finally, she cut his hair and Samson was powerless when his captors attacked. *Lord, I will "crucify" or put to death my lust of the flesh before it puts me to death.*

But his strength was not in his hair, it was in the Lord. He lied so many times and compromised so often, that when he finally explained the divine symbol of his strength; it was the last straw. But he was so blinded with sin; he didn't know when he crossed the line. When Samson's hair was cut, his link to God was cut. What is the final straw in your life? *Lord, I am horrified at the thought of crossing it.*

God loves symbols, because they outwardly represent His inner work. And when you violate God's symbol, you spit in God's face. What are some of today's symbols? Baptism, the Lord's Table, the Cross, the Lord's Day, etc. *Lord, I love Your symbols and reverence them.*

Samson was spiritually blinded before the Philistines physically blinded him. "He didn't know the Spirit of God had left him." How can God's presence leave and you not know it? If you're walking through a crowd, your partner can unknowingly walk away from you if you're looking away, not paying attention, or distracted. If you're looking for someone else, you might lose the one you're with. Have you lost God's presence? How long has the Lord been gone before you missed Him? If you met Him daily, it would be a short time, and little damage would have been done. Keeping His presence in your life requires constant attention. You must give the Lord your undivided attention, 24/7. *Lord, I will pay attention to You.*

My Time to Pray

Lord, I realize Samson was Your follower
Because his name is listed in
The Hall of Faith (see Heb. 11:32).

So Samson didn't lose his salvation because
  Of his sin, he went to Heaven.

Lord, I don't understand why You use a sinning saint,
  But then, all believers sin (see 1 Tim. 1:15);
  So it's mercy that You use even me.

Keep me from inner and outer sin;
  I don't want to sin against You,
  Nor do I want to destroy Your testimony.

Lord, I would rather You bring me home with You
  Rather than allow me to sin openly,
  Keep me from sin.

  Amen.

Micah's Idols

SCRIPTURE: JUDGES 17

There was a man whose name was Micah, who lived in the hill-country of Ephraim. And Micah admitted to his mother, "Your 1,100 pieces of silver are missing. When it was lost, you uttered a curse of God upon the one who took it. I heard that curse with my own ears. Well…I stole it. Look, mother, I was the one who took it." *Lord, stealing is always wrong, even from relatives.*

His mother said, "I hereby utter a blessing from the Lord on you, my son."

Micah gave the 1,100 silver pieces back to his mother. Then his mother said, "From my hand, I hereby totally consecrate this silver to You, O Lord my God. I will have my son make a carved image and an idol of melted silver to You. So now I am giving it back to You." (In her pagan ignorance, the mother thought that her "consecration" of this silver would benefit her son. This mother probably saved up all of this silver to give to her son as an inheritance.) Micah gave the silver to his mother, and she took 200 pieces of silver and gave them to the idolmaker. The idol-maker made a carved image and an idol of melted silver. This shrine was kept in Micah's house.

Micah had his own little temple for worshiping idols. (Micah was adopting pagan practices in a kind of syncretistic worship of Yahweh.) Micah made a special holy vest ("an ephod") for a priest. Then Micah consecrated one of his own sons to be his priest. (This investiture of a non-Levitical priest was a direct violation of the Law of Moses (see Exod. 29:35; Lev. 8:33; Num.

3:10.)) In those days, the Israelites did not have a king. So everyone did what he thought was right. *Lord, it's never right to do the wrong thing for a good purpose.*

There was a young man who was a Levite, a grandson of Moses himself from the town of Bethlehem-in-Judah. (This young Levite was previously associated with the tribe of Judah, on his mother's side, accounting for his being in Bethlehem, which was not one of the Levitical cities.) He left Bethlehem-in-Judah to look for another place to live. On his way, he came to Micah's house, in the hill-country of Ephraim. Micah asked him, "Where have you come from?" He answered, "I am a Levite from Bethlehem-in-Judah, and I am looking for a place to live." Then Micah said, "Live with me. Be my spiritual father and my priest. I will give you ten pieces of silver each year. I will also provide all of your clothes and your food." The young Levite agreed to live with Micah, and became to Micah like one of his own sons. *Lord, no one can properly serve God contrary to God's chosen way of service.*

Micah ordained him as his priest; the Levite lived in Micah's house. Then Micah said, "Now I know that the Lord will be good to me. I know this because I have a Levite as my priest." (It is strange that his idolatrous worship occurred in the vicinity of Shiloh, where God's true Tabernacle was located.) *Lord, may I always worship You in the right way with the right heart attitude.*

Micah and the Tribe of Dan

SCRIPTURE: JUDGES 18

At that time, the Israelites did not have a king. The tribe of Dan was
    still looking for a land-inheritance where they might settle.

The other tribes of Israel already had received their own territories, but
    the Danites had not yet gotten their own land. So the Danites
    sent out five soldiers from all of their clans. These five men were
    from the cities of Zorah and Eshtaol. The Danites sent the men
    to spy out and explore the land. They told the five men, "Go,
    explore the land." So the five men came to the hill-country of
    Ephraim, Micah's house, where they spent the night. When they
    came to Micah's house, they recognized the voice of the young
    Levite. (He had a southern accent. Perhaps they even knew him
    from before, since he was famous—he was Moses' grandson.)
    They asked the young Levite, "Who brought you here? What are
    you doing at this place? Why are you here?" He told them
    everything that Micah had done for him: "He has hired me; I am
    his priest." *Lord, I will not follow a minister who serves contrary
    to Your commandments and plan of worship.*

They said to him, "Please, on our behalf, ask God this question: We
    want to know if our search for a place to settle will be success-
    ful?" The priest said to them, "Go in peace. The Lord is pleased
    with your journey." *Lord, I want my friends to tell me the truth,
    not what I want to hear.*

So the five men left, and came to the city of Laish. They saw that the
    people lived there safely. They were like the people of Sidon, a
    quiet people, and they were not afraid. They had an abundance

of everything. Yet, they lived far away from the Sidonians and had no relationship with anyone else.

The five men went back to their Danite brothers at Zorah and Eshtaol, where they were asked, "What did you find out?" They answered, "We have seen the land, it is very good! We should attack them. Why hesitate? Don't wait. Let's go and capture that land. When you arrive, you will see that there is plenty of land. There is plenty of everything. The people are not expecting us to attack. Surely God has given this land to us?" *Lord, teach me to think and see before I act.*

So 600 men of the tribe of Dan left Zorah and Eshtaol, ready for war. (Numbers 26:43 states that they had 64,400 males who were 20 years old or older.) On their way, they camped near the city of Kiriath-Jearim in Judah west of Kiriath-Jearim. That is why the place is named Mahaneh-Dan (Dan's camp) to this very day. From there, they traveled on to the hill-country of Ephraim, then they came to Micah's house. So the five men who had gone to explore the land said to their Danite brothers, "There is a special vest for a priest in one of these houses, and there are household gods. There is also a carved image and an idol of melted silver. You know what to do." So they stopped at the Levite's house and entered it, (this was also Micah's house) and greeted the Levite. The 600 Danite men stood at the entrance of the gate, wearing their weapons of war.

The five spies went into the house, took the carved image, the special vest for a priest, the household idols, and the silver idol. The 600 men ready for war stood guard at the entrance of the gate, along with the Levite. When the spies went into Micah's house and took the religious things, the priest asked them, "What are you doing?" They answered, "Be quiet, don't say a word. Come with us. Be our father and our priest. It is better for you to be a priest for a tribe and clan than to be a priest for the people for one man's household." Then the priest was glad in his heart. So he took the special vest for a priest, the household idols, and the carved image, and he went with the men of Dan. *Lord, nothing good can come of lying, deceit, and stealing.*

As they left Micah's house, they put their little children, their animals, and everything they owned in front of them. (Perhaps this Levite's central position in the march was an imitation of the spot appointed for the priests when Israel came out of Egypt.) The men of Dan traveled a long way from Micah's house. Then the men who lived near Micah's house were called to chase the men of Dan. When they caught up with them, they shouted at the men of Dan. The men of Dan turned around and said to Micah, "What's the matter with you? Why have you called out your men to fight?"

Micah answered, "You took my idols. I made them. You took my priest, too. What else do I have? How can you say to me, 'What's the matter with you?'"

The Danites answered, "You should not argue with us, some of our men have hot tempers. If you shout at us, they might attack you. You and your family might be killed." Then the Danites went on their way. Micah knew that they were too strong for him. So he turned and went back home. *Lord, teach me to back down when the battle is too big to win and the results inconsequential.*

So the men of Dan took what Micah had made. They also took his priest. When they arrived at Laish, they attacked those peaceful people. The people of Laish did not expect an attack, so the men of Dan killed them with their swords. Then they set the city on fire. There was no one to save the people of Laish; they lived too far from Sidon, and they had no relationship with anyone else. Laish was in a valley near Beth-Rehob. The people of Dan rebuilt the city in that place, and settled there.

They changed the name of Laish to "Dan" after their ancestor, Dan. He was one of the sons of Israel. *Lord, a new name doesn't "sanctify" the evil that Dan did to Laish.*

The Danites set up the idol for themselves. (They didn't feel the need to go to God's Tabernacle at Shiloh; theirs was a tribal heresy.) They made Jonathan their priest, the son of Gershom, and the grandson of Moses. Jonathan and his sons were priests for the tribe of the Danites. (They served as priests until the Israelites were taken captive.) The people of Dan worshiped the idol which Micah had made, all during the time that the Tabernacle of the one true God was at Shiloh. *Lord, I will worship You properly, not as some who worship improperly.*

Judges 18

The Story of Three Carnal Mistakes

Date: 1406 B.C. ⌒ Place: Dan

Then five men (spies from Dan)...came to Laish and saw the people that were there, how they dwelt carelessly, after the manner of the Sidonions, quiet and secure; and there was no magistrate, and they had no business with any man...they came to Laish, to a people who were quiet and secure, and they smote them with the edge of the sword, and burned the city with fire (Judges 18:7,27-28).

Sin is never an isolated act or attitude, like the adultery it fosters; sin has children, grandchildren, and great grandchildren. Sin never stops with one act, or one look, or one incidence. Those who purposely commit adultery never do it just once. *Lord, help me fear the grandchildren of sin.*

The first carnal mistake: Micah wanted the blessings of God on his home. But you can't bless the right thing on the wrong basis. He stole his mother's silver, he made an idol and an ephod that a priest used to find the will of God. Then he built a shrine in his house. All this is contrary to God's "man" and God's "place." *Lord, teach me to be afraid of compromising Your plan of worship.*

Jonathan—the grandson of Moses—was hired to be Micah's private priest. Doesn't that sound arrogant? Shouldn't Jonathan have remembered the standards of his grandfather Moses? Did Jonathan think he could create his own following just as his grandfather Moses? *Lord, this also sounds arrogant.*

The second carnal mistake was made by the Danites when they learned about the ephod, the idol, and the "priest" when they chose to lodge in the home of Micah. To demonstrate their gratitude, they returned to steal the ephod, the idol, and "the priest Jonathan." *Lord, no one can "steal" the presence of God.*

The Danites then go on their murderous way. They completely destroy the people of Laish, killing, burning, and wiping out all human life. Can the Danites be described as godly invaders? No! Did God allot them this land as their land-inheritance? No! These Danites make a carnal mistake that will stay with them as long as they are in the land. The Danites were always one of the weakest tribes in Israel.

The third mistake was made by the people of Laish. They were careless in their supposed security. They kept no guard, they had never needed a guard, and they lived in a "fool's paradise." They didn't understand the times nor the culture in which they lived. They didn't realize it was a dog-eat-dog world, and that Joshua had annihilated other tribes to the south of them. *Lord, help me be vigilant against sin.*

There are many believers who live like Laish; they think the devil is dead, that they are no longer tossed about by the waves of heresy, and that this earthly life is peaceful like Heaven. God help us remember, most people are lost in the calm before the storm because they didn't prepare for the storm, then are lost in the storm itself.

When the Bible says, "There was no magistrate in the land," it means the people of Dan had learned to live with themselves. They didn't need a judge to determine the law. Isn't that like today's religious sleepy believers who don't know the dangers about them? Just as Laish needed a judge, today we need men and women of God to warn us of our drift toward complacency and the gradual advance of sleep. *Lord, thank You for bold preachers who warn me of danger.*

One of the weaknesses of Laish was self-confidence. "Soul, take your ease, you have much goods laid up for many years—eat, drink, be merry."

Laish got along with everyone. No quarrels, no fights, no problems. When everyone likes the believers and they like everyone, there is a problem. Jesus taught that if the world hated Him, it would hate His followers also. So if no one hates you for your Christian stand, then you are not safe; you're on thin ice, in danger of losing everything. *Lord, I don't like it when people don't like me, but it's then when I realize my love for You causes them to hate me.*

There's nothing wrong with living in peace like the people of Laish. There's nothing wrong with peace, contentment, and respect of others. It's when you're deceived about the enemy and you're deluded about sin, and you're no longer on guard—that's when you're in the most danger. *Lord, I will keep watch over my soul and be on guard against the world, the flesh and the devil.*

The Levite and His Concubine

SCRIPTURE: JUDGES 19

At that time, the people of Israel did not have a king. There was a Levite
man who lived in the far side of the hill-country of Ephraim. He
had taken a concubine-wife, from the town of Bethlehem-in-
Judah. But she was unfaithful to him. She left him and went
back to her father's house in Bethlehem-in-Judah. She stayed
there for a long time—four months. Then her husband got up
and went after her. He wanted to persuade her to return. He
took with him his servant boy and a team of donkeys. The Levite
arrived at her father's house, and she invited him in. When her
father saw his son-in-law, he gladly welcomed him. He asked the
Levite to stay. So the Levite intended to stay with him for only
three days. The Levite ate, drank, and slept there. *Lord, how can
a man of God who has sex outside the will of God have Your
blessing on his life and ministry?*

On the fourth day, they got up early in the morning. The Levite was getting ready to leave, but the woman's father said to his son-in-
law, "Refresh yourself by eating something. Then you may
travel." So the two men sat down to eat and drink together. After
that, the young woman's father said to him, "Please stay tonight.
Relax, and enjoy yourself." When the Levite man got up to go,
his father-in-law urged him to stay longer. So the Levite stayed
again that night. On the fifth day, the man got up early in the
morning to leave. The young woman's father said, "Refresh yourself. Wait until this afternoon." So the two men ate together.

Then the Levite, his concubine-wife, and his servant boy got up to leave.
His father-in-law said to the Levite, "It's almost night. The day is

almost gone. So spend the night here and enjoy yourself. Tomorrow morning, you may get up early for your trip and go on home." But the Levite did not want to stay another night. He took his two saddled donkeys and his concubine-wife, and traveled toward the city of Jebus. (Jebus is another name for Jerusalem.) The day was almost over as they came near Jebus. So the servant boy said to his master, "Let's stop here. It's the city of the Jebusite people. Let's spend the night in there." But the Levite said, "No, we won't go inside that strange city. Those people are not Israelites. We will go on to the city of Gibeah." Then he said to the boy, "Come on, let's try to make it to Gibeah or Ramah. We can spend the night in one of those towns." So they traveled on. The sun had gone down when they came near Gibeah. (Gibeah belongs to the tribe of Benjamin.) So they stopped in Gibeah to spend the night. They went to the public square in the middle of the town and sat down. But no one invited them home to spend the night. (Since there were no public inns in which to stay, it was the custom of travelers—those who had no invitation to spend the night in a private home—to spread out their bedding in the streets or wrap themselves up in their robes and pass the night in the open air.) *Lord, help me realize when it is best to stop and rest, rather than "pressing on" against common sense.*

That evening an old man came into the town from his work in the fields. He was living in Gibeah. Looking up, he saw the traveler—the Levite man—in the public square. The old man asked, "Where are you going? Where did you come from?" The Levite answered, "We are traveling from Bethlehem-in-Judah. We are headed home. I am from the hill-country of Ephraim, far away. Though I have been to Bethlehem-in-Judah, I am now going to the Tabernacle of God. No one has invited me to stay in his house. We already have straw and feed for our donkeys. Also, there is bread and wine for me, for the concubine-wife, and for my servant. We don't need anything."

The old man said, "No, you are welcome to stay at my house. Let me give you anything you need. But don't spend the night in the public square." So the old man took the Levite into his home. He fed their donkeys, and the servants washed their feet. Then they ate some food and had something to drink. *Lord, teach me hospitality.*

While they were enjoying themselves, some very evil men (sons of Belial) of the city surrounded the house. They pounded on the door, and shouted to the old men who owned the house, saying, "Bring out the man who has come into your house. We want to have sex with him!" *Lord, evil comes in many different ways; help me recognize it and protect myself.*

The owner of the house went outside to them, and said, "No, my brothers. Please, don't be so vile. This man is a guest in my house. Don't do this shameful thing. Look, here is my daughter. She is a virgin. And here is the man's concubine-wife. Let me bring them out to you now. Do anything you want with them. Humiliate them, but don't do such a terrible thing to this man." *Lord, a "lesser sin" is not any better in God's eyes than a "greater sin." May I never bargain with sin.*

But the men would not listen to him. So the old man seized the concubine-wife and put her outside with them. And they raped her, abusing her all night long. Then at dawn, they let her go. She came back to the house where her master was staying, and fell down at the door and lay there until daylight.

In the morning the Levite got up and opened the door of the house. He stepped outside to go on his way, but he saw the woman, his concubine-wife, lying there. She had fallen down at the doorway of the house. Her hands were on the threshold. Then the Levite said to her, "Get up; let's go." But she didn't answer, she was dead. So he put her on his donkey and went home. *Lord, remind me that going against common sense and compromise leads to terrible results.*

When the Levite got home, he took a knife and cut his concubine up into 12 parts, bone by bone. Then he sent a piece to each of the territories where the people of Israel lived. (He was attempting to incite a general horror and sense of outrage in all of Israel. It was a dramatic call to arms to rectify this moral breach which occurred within the territory of Benjamin.) Everyone who saw this said, "Nothing like this has ever happened before. It has never happened since the people of Israel came up out of the land of Egypt. Think about it. Talk to each other about this, and take action." *Lord, help me realize that disobedience and small sins lead to horrible consequences.*

Judges 19

The Story of the Levite's Compromise Over His Concubine

Date: 1406 B.C. ⌁ Place: Gibeah

When a person intentionally breaks one of God's foundational laws, they usually don't stop at one, they break a lot more. Sometimes it's like slipping on the first stair, that slip starts a fall that results in a lot of painful bumps and damaging crashes before reaching the bottom of all the stairs. *Lord, I've fallen down spiritual stairs before and I don't want to do it again.*

What makes that first transgression so crucial, is that the person thinks he knows better than God, or he thinks God doesn't mean it when He warns us of danger. *Lord, I believe You and will steer clear of danger.*

The Levite should know God's law better than anyone else, because he ministers for God. He should know about the dreaded seventh, because of its ramifications that will destroy him and his ministry. But no, he had a concubine. Now the original language could be translated "slave wife," meaning they acted like a married couple, without a ceremony. The only ceremony he went through was buying her. As a matter of fact, isn't buying a woman for sex called prostitution? *Lord, give me wisdom to always stop at Your STOP signs.*

Maybe God was trying to get the Levite out of his affair. His concubine left him and went home to her parents. The Levite should have left well enough alone. He should have cut his losses and walked away. But he went to get her. Why? Maybe it was the money he paid for her. Maybe it was the sex. It sure wasn't love because of the brutal way he treated her; he even let her be thrown out of a house to a mob of sexual deviates— homosexuals and lustful maniacs. They ravished her all night. *Lord, protect me from sexual deviates.*

When the Levite got to his concubine's parent's home, the father-in-law used a bunch of stalling tactics to keep him there. Maybe the Levite should have seen his concubine had more attachment to her parents, than to him. *Lord, I know You lead me through relationships, help me read rightly all my relationships.*

Then the Levite left in the late afternoon—bad timing. He should have used his common sense in this decision. As a result he ended up in Gibeah going to sleep in the city square. Maybe the Levite got there too late to get a decent invitation to someone's home. *Lord, help me find Your perfect will for my life by not going against common sense, especially when it agrees with Scripture.*

An old man came out from his field working late at night. The square would have been dangerous at night, as the latter case reveals. It was then when the sexual deviates came to the front door demanding sex with the Levite. This was a predicament the Levite should have never gotten himself into. The old man went out and offered his virgin daughter and the concubine to the deviates. *Lord, save the world from sexual deviates for they will destroy all decency if they have their own way.*

When all else failed, the old man threw the concubine to the deviates. Where was the Levite? Was he "too godly" to get a stick to beat away the deviates? Did he go to see about her, or did he only "thank God" for his safety? *Lord, give me courage to fight to the death to defend the decency of any woman under attack.*

The next morning when the Levite opened the door to get the morning paper to read, he found his concubine dead—molested to death. Did he bury her body? No. Did he return the body to her parents, apparently the only ones who cared for her? No! *Lord, may I always be touched deeply with the death of any of Your children.*

If the Levite were living today, he might use an unfortunate murder for political purpose—television time. The Levite has rage against the Benjamites and instigates a civil war of 11 tribes against this small tribe. *Lord, remind me that my inward sins of lust and outward sins of compromise can have huge consequences.*

This story should warn us of inner sin and outer sin. Also it tells us that when we know to do good, but do it not, it is sin (see James 4:17). Finally, the Levite transferred his guilt—if he had any—to the nation. When each tribe received a "chopped up body part," their rage and guilt flamed into civil war. All of that might have been prohibited if the Levite had conscientiously obeyed God, "Thou shall not commit adultery" (Seventh Commandment). *Lord, I will obey the Seventh.*

Israelites Punish the Benjaminites for Their Sin

SCRIPTURE: JUDGES 20

So all the Israelites joined together. They stood in the presence of the Lord in the city of Mizpah. They came from as far away as the cities of Dan and Beer-Sheba. (A proverbial expression for the extreme north and the extreme south of the land of Israel.) Even Israelites from the land of Gilead were there. The top leaders of all the tribes of Israel were there (except the tribe of Benjamin). They took their places in the meeting of the people of God. There were 400,000 infantry with swords. The people of Benjamin heard that the Israelites had gone up to Mizpah. Then the Israelites said to the Levite man, "Tell us, how did this evil thing happen?"

So the husband of the murdered woman answered: "My concubine-wife and I came to Gibeah, which belongs to the territory of Benjamin, to spend the night. During the night, the men of Gibeah came after me, surrounding the house; they intended to kill me and my concubine-wife. They raped her, and she died. So I grabbed my concubine-wife and cut her up into 12 parts. Then I sent one piece to each territory of Israel. Why? Because the people of Benjamin have done this disgraceful and terrible thing in Israel. All of you sons of Israel, speak up. Tell us what you have decided we should do here." *Lord, a compromised leader rallies a crowd to terrible actions that are not blessed by You.*

Then all of the people stood up at the same time, and said, "None of us will go back home. Not one of us will go back to his house until we have punished the guilty ones of Gibeah. Now, this is what we will do to Gibeah. We will pick lots, so that God can show us what to do. We will choose ten men from each set of 100 men. They will be from each set of 1,000 men. We will choose 1,000 men from each set of 10,000 men. These men will find supplies for the army. Then the army will go to the city of Gibeah of Benjamin. They will repay those people for the terrible thing that they have done in Israel." So all the men of Israel gathered against the city of Gibeah. They all agreed about what they were going to accomplish.

The tribes of Israel sent men to all the clans of Benjamin with this message: "What about this awful crime which some of your Benjaminite men have done? Surrender these evil men in Gibeah, so that we can put them to death. We must remove this evil from Israel." *Lord, the principle was to punish the guilty, not punish everyone.*

But the Benjaminites would not listen to their Hebrew brothers, the people of Israel. (By not surrendering the few guilty homosexuals for execution because of the rape [see Deut. 22:22], all the Benjaminites became a party to the actions of the perpetrators.)

The Benjaminites gathered together out of their own towns and met at Gibeah. They went to fight against the Israelites. In only one day, the Benjaminites mobilized 26,000 soldiers out of their towns. These soldiers were trained with swords. They also had 700 select men living in Gibeah. Seven hundred of these trained soldiers were left-handed. Each of them could sling a stone at a hair and not miss. (They could hurl a rock as much as 200 yards with great velocity.)

The Israelites—except for the Benjaminites—gathered 400,000 fighting men. These 400,000 men were trained soldiers to use swords. The Israelites went up to the city of Bethel. The Israelites asked

God: "Which tribe will be first to attack the Benjaminites?" The Lord answered, "Judah will go up first." The next morning, the Israelites got up and encamped against Gibeah. Then the men of Israel went out to fight the Benjaminites. The Israelites got into battle position against Gibeah.

Then the Benjaminites came out of Gibeah. On that day, the Benjaminites killed 22,000 Israelites on the battlefield. The Israelites went into the presence of the Lord, and wept until the evening. They asked the Lord: "Should we go fight our Hebrew brothers, the Benjaminites, again?" *Lord, sometimes You "test" us with defeat.*

And the Lord answered, "Go up and fight against them." The Israelite army took courage. So they occupied the same battle positions which they had taken up the first day. The Israelites drew closer to the Benjaminites on the second day. The Benjaminites came out of Gibeah to attack the Israelites on the second day. This time, the Benjaminites killed 18,000 Israelites on the battlefield. And all of these men had been trained with swords.

Then the entire Israelite army went up to Bethel. There they sat down and wept in the presence of the Lord. They fasted (to go without food and pray for a period of time, usually for spiritual reasons) all day until the evening. They also offered whole burnt offerings and peace offerings to the Lord. The Israelites asked the Lord a question. In those days, the Ark of the Covenant of the one true God was there at Bethel. In those days, Phinehas (the high priest) was serving in the presence of the Lord before the Ark. He was the son of Eleazar, who was the son of Aaron. (This line of text helps us to understand the chronology. It was shortly after the death of Joshua.) The people of Israel asked the Lord, "Should we go to fight against our Hebrew brothers, the Benjaminites again? Or should we stop fighting?" The Lord answered, "Go up, because tomorrow I will hand them over to you." *Lord, prayer without blood sacrifice will not lead to success.*

Then the Israelites hid some men all around Gibeah. The Israelites set themselves in battle array against the Benjaminites at Gibeah on the third day. They got into their positions for doing battle, the same as they had done before. Then the Benjaminites came out of the city to fight the army. The Israelites retreated, leading the Benjaminites away from the city. The Benjaminites began to strike down some of the Israelite army, as they had done before. About 30 men of Israel were killed—some on the roads and some in the fields. One road led to Bethel. Another road led to Gibeah. The Benjaminites thought: "We are winning, just as before!" The Israelites had said, "Let's run. Let's trick them into going farther away from the city and onto the roads." *Lord, strength in battle is not enough, there must be a good strategy.*

Then all the men of Israel jumped up from their places. They got into battle positions at a place called Baal-Tamar. Then the Israelites ran out of their hiding places, even out of Maareh-Geba. Ten thousand of the best trained soldiers from the entire army of Israel attacked Gibeah. This third army that attacked the city is to be distinguished from the main army and the other division which was ready to ambush the Benjaminites. The battle was very hard. The Benjaminites did not know that a disaster was about to happen to them. The Lord used the Israelites to strike down the Benjaminites. (This verse gives a general account of the war, but Judges 20:36-48 gives a detailed narrative of the battle.) On that day, the Israelites killed 25,100 Benjaminites. All of these men were trained with swords. Then the Benjaminites saw that they were defeated.

The main army of Israel had moved back, away from the Benjaminites. They had retreated because they were depending on the surprise ambush which they had set up against the city of Gibeah. Then the men in ambush jumped up and rushed into Gibeah. They spread out and killed everybody in town with their swords. Now the main army of Israel had made a plan with the men in the ambush that they were to send up a signal—a big cloud of smoke rising from the city. So that's when the main army of Israel saw the smoke, they turned around in the battle.

The Benjaminites had killed about 30 Israelites, thinking: "We are winning, just as in the first battle." But then the big column of smoke began to rise from the city. The Benjaminites turned around and saw it. The whole city was going up in smoke. Then the Israelites turned on them and began to fight. And the Benjaminites were terrified. They realized that disaster was about to happen to them. So the Benjaminites ran away from the Israelites. They ran toward the desert, but they could not escape the battle. Then the Israelites who came out of the towns killed the Benjaminites. They surrounded the Benjaminites and chased them without letting up. They caught the Benjaminites in the area which is east of Gibeah. So 18,000 strong Benjaminite fighters were killed. Some of the Benjaminites ran toward the desert. They ran to a place called "the Rock of Rimmon" (a place of refuge among the caves of these rugged mountains). But the Israelites killed 5,000 Benjaminites along the roads. They kept chasing them as far as a place named Gidom. And they struck down 2,000 more Benjaminites there.

On that day, 25,000 Benjaminite soldiers were killed. (About 1,100 men are unaccounted for.) All of these men were brave soldiers. *Lord, it's always sad when any are killed in battle.*

But 600 surviving Benjaminite men turned and ran off to the Rock of Rimmon in the desert. They stayed there for four months. Then the men of Israel worked their way back against the Benjaminites. They used their swords to kill the Benjaminites in every town. They also killed the animals, destroying everything they could find. (God had not sanctioned the extermination of the tribe of Benjamin.) And every town that they could find they set on fire. *Lord, the leaders of Benjamin made a foolish decision, and everyone paid a price. Help me make smart decisions for those I lead.*

Wives for the Benjaminites

SCRIPTURE: JUDGES 21

At Mizpah, the men of Israel had made a vow: "Not one of us will
allow his daughter to marry a man from the tribe of Benjamin."
The army went to the city of Bethel, and sat in the presence of
God (at the Tabernacle) until the evening, crying loudly. They
said, "O Lord God, You are the God of Israel. Why has this terrible thing happened in our nation? Why should one tribe be
missing from Israel today?" *Lord, the people who slaughtered
Benjamin are now mourning their loss. May I never be so
hypocritical.*

The next day, the people got up early and built an altar and offered
whole burnt offerings and peace offerings to God. Then the
Israelites asked, "Was there any group within Israel that failed to
assemble here before the Lord?" They asked this question
because they had made a great vow, that anyone who did not
come up to meet with them at Mizpah would surely be killed.

The Israelites felt sorry for their Hebrew brothers, the Benjaminites.
They said, "Today, one tribe has been cut off from Israel. We
made a vow by the Lord that we would not allow our daughters
to marry a Benjaminite. But how can we make sure that the
remaining men of Benjamin will have wives?" (This question
was addressed to their fellow Israelites, not to God.) Then they
asked, "Which group of Israel did not come here to the Lord at
Mizpah?" And, look, no one from the city of Jabesh-Gilead was
there in the assembly. They did a roll call of the army of Israel
and found there was not a single resident of Jabesh-Gilead present in Mizpah.

So the whole group of Israelites sent 12,000 powerful soldiers to
Jabesh-Gilead. They ordered the soldiers to kill the people in
Jabesh-Gilead with their swords. Even the women and children
were to be killed. (This human action did not come from seeking
God's counsel.) "This is what you must do: Kill every man in
Jabesh-Gilead. Also, kill every woman who has had sex with a
man." The soldiers found 400 young women in Jabesh-Gilead
who had never had sex with a man. They brought these women
to the camp at Shiloh, which is in the land of Canaan. *Lord, this
is terrible justice.*

Then the whole group of Israelites sent a message to the men of
Benjamin, who were at the Rock of Rimmon. The Israelites
offered amnesty to them. So the men of Benjamin came back at
that time. The Israelites gave them the virgins from Jabesh-
Gilead whom they had kept alive. However, there were still not
enough women for all of the Benjaminites. *Lord, I don't understand how the people thought in that day. May I always think
biblically.*

The people of Israel felt sorry for the Benjaminites. This was because
the Lord had made a gap among the tribes of Israel. The elders
of the Jewish community said, "All the women of the tribe of
Benjamin have been killed. Where are we going to get more
wives for the rest of the Benjaminite men?" They added, "These
surviving men must have children to continue their families (The
men of Benjamin were the only rightful owners of this territory
of Benjamin. Therefore, they had to have the means to transmit
it to their legitimate heirs in the future. The situation was urgent
so that a tribe in Israel will not die out.). Nevertheless, we cannot allow our daughters to marry them because we made this
vow: 'Anyone who gives a wife to a man of Benjamin will be
cursed.'" Then the elders said, "We've got an idea. There is a
yearly festival of the Lord at Shiloh. Shiloh is north of the city of

Bethel. It is east of the road that goes up from Bethel to Shechem. And it is south of the town of Lebonah."

So the elders told the men of Benjamin about their idea. They said, "Go and hide in the vineyards. Watch for the virgins of Shiloh to come out to join in the dancing with the other girls. Then you men should jump out from the vineyards. Let each man grab one virgin of the daughters of Shiloh to be his wife. Then go to the land of Benjamin. *Lord, I'm glad we don't choose wives this way today.*

"The fathers or brothers of those virgins will come to us. They will complain, but we will say: 'Be gracious to the men of Benjamin. We did not get enough wives for Benjamin during the war. And you did not knowingly give the women to the Benjaminites. So you are not guilty!'" *Lord, this is twisted logic.*

So that is exactly what the Benjaminites did. While the virgins were dancing, each man caught one of them. They took them away and married them. Then they went back to their land-inheritance and rebuilt their towns, and settled in them.

Then at that time, the Israelites went home. Each one went to his own tribe and clan. They left there, each man to go to his own land-inheritance.

In those days, the Israelites did not have a king. Everyone did what he thought was right. *Lord, the Bible is accurate, "Each man did what he thought was right," but so often, he (or they) was wrong. Lord, may I do what is right according to the Bible.*

My Time to Pray

Lord, these "Dark Ages" of Israel were terrible;
People lived contrary to Your law,
They were often wrong and suffered for it.

Lord, teach me to live according to what You've revealed
As Your standard in the Word of God.

Lord, many of the people thought they were doing right
When actually they were foolishly wrong.

Lord, I know that sincerity and prayer are not enough
To live and serve You correctly;
I will live by Your law in the Bible.

Amen.

PRAYING RUTH
TO SEE GOD'S SOVEREIGN HAND

INTRODUCTION

O ld Samuel finished writing the Book of Judges. He didn't like what he wrote for the book described 300 years of moral blackness and corruption. Samuel didn't like writing about a Levitical priest with a live-in concubine. He cringed at the thought of God using a womanizing Samson, or a half-breed Jephthah, or a reluctant Gideon, or a henpecked Othniel. But worse than fleshly sins was the religious corruption and heresy of Micah and his private Levite-priest and private "tabernacle."

Samuel wanted to weep over the message of Judges, but God spoke to him, "Remember Ruth."

"Yes," Samuel's eyes twinkled. The thought of Ruth reminded him of David, a man after God's own heart. Samuel had anointed David as king and knew in his heart David would restore righteousness to Israel. Samuel had listened to David sing Psalms while playing the harp and knew God would restore spirituality to Israel. The old priest prayed, *"Thank You, Lord, for David."*

David's great grandmother was Ruth. Her godliness was poured into her son Obed, and then into her grandson Jesse, the father of David. "Yes," Samuel thought, "I'll write about Ruth, but I won't include her story in the Judges. She is a light shining in darkness, a love story among corruption and debauchery."

Samuel wrote the first line of his new book, "Now it came to pass in the days when the judges ruled that there was a famine" (Ruth 1:1). A young scribe looked over Samuel's shoulder to ask, "When did Ruth live?"

Samuel didn't give a straight answer, but remarked, "There were 300 years of Judges from the death of Joshua to Saul the first king" (see Judg. 11:26). Then the old Samuel answered, "Ruth lived at the beginning when

Judges first ruled Israel, over 300 years ago. She lived about 1410 B.C. during the time of the first Judge, Othniel."

"How do you know?" the young scholar asked.

Samuel put his finger to his head to show he was thinking, then said, "Ruth's husband—Boaz—was the son of Rahab the harlot. Rahab came to faith when Joshua destroyed Jericho. Solomon married her and their son was Boaz." Then Samuel concluded, "Ruth lived about 40 years from the beginning of Judges."

Again the scribe asked, "Why didn't you include her story in Judges?"

Samuel laughed. "You don't put clean water in a dirty pot, and the story of Ruth is too pure to include with the problem of the Judges."

Then Samuel returned to his private thoughts. "Rahab was a Gentile prostitute who turned to Jehovah, and Ruth was a Gentile widow who also turned to the Lord; two tokens that the God of Abraham would bless Gentiles who turned to Him."

Samuel wanted everyone to know that Ruth, a pagan girl from Moab, made a life-changing decision to follow the God of Israel. Her decision to follow the Lord God was also a decision to reject Molek, Moab's god, and the false gods across the Jordan River. When Ruth said, "Your people shall be my people," she said "no" to her heathen relatives and their idolatrous culture. When God saw the deep faith of Ruth, He must have thought, "I want that girl in the physical lineage to my Son Jesus." *Lord, thank You for Ruth's choice so that the Messiah—Jesus Christ—came from her line.*

The Book of Ruth is a story of exemplary love that grew out of good choices. In a day when so many girls make bad choices—about friends, habits, listening and viewing entertainment, also about drugs, alcohol, tobacco, etc.—it's refreshing to see the wise choices of Ruth. *Lord, keep me from making bad choices.*

Ruth chose the Lord God over the false gods chosen by Orpah. Ruth chose a Jewish family and a Jewish culture over the debauchery of Moab. She chose to honor her mother-in-law and work hard. Then God rewarded her in grace. Hebrews tells us, "without faith it is impossible to please

Him...you must believe that God exists and is a rewarder of those who diligently seek Him" (Heb. 11:6). *Lord, reward me for my diligence to seek Your presence in my life.*

This is the 38th book of the Bible I've translated into *Praying the Scriptures*. May your faith grow as you read this transliteration of the wonderfully written masterpiece we call simply, *Ruth*.

> *Lord, give me the faith of Ruth as I pray the story of her faith journey, and may my faith reward me with Your blessing, as You rewarded Ruth.*

Sincerely yours in Christ,
Elmer Towns
Written from my home
At the foot of the Blue Ridge Mountains

The Story of the Book of Ruth

DATE: 1322 B.C. ⁊ PLACE: MOAB

Elimelech stood out in a crowd because of his self-importance. When he sat by the city well, someone quickly brought him a cup of water because he expected it. When he walked the narrow street, people moved aside to let him pass, because Elimelech never considered getting out of anyone's way. He was called an "Ephrathites of Bethlehem" (Ruth 1:2), meaning a blue blood whose family were original settlers of the town.

When famine ravaged the area, Elimelech lived better than the rest of the town because of stored-up wealth. The following year seeds dried up in the ground for lack of rain; parched grass and bushes didn't bloom. Then Elimelech's cash dried up. God was punishing the area because Israel began intermarrying with the heathen tribes around them. Rather than repenting and praying to the Lord God, Israel began praying to heathen gods to see if their god could do what they thought Jehovah couldn't do. *Lord, help me observe nature through Your plan and eyes.*

From the top of tall hills in Bethlehem, Elimelech could look out over the Dead Sea to the green hills of Moab 40 miles away. "Plenty of green grass is Moab," Elimelech announced to his family. Then without discussion, he moved to Moab, choosing with the eye of necessity, not the heart of faith of his ancestors who settled in Bethlehem.

Elimelech didn't plan to settle down in Moab, "We'll live in tents till this famine is over," he told Naomi his wife. But within months they built a house and began to prosper again. Some people who backslide from God actually prosper. As he dressed like his new friends and gave up his Jewish ways, Elimelech was asked to sit in the city gate. His two sons Mahlon (meaning sickly) and Chilion (meaning pining) each found a Moabite girl to marry. *Lord, I'd rather be poor in the center of Your will then to have riches outside Your plan for my life.*

Elimelech knew God told Israel not to intermarry, but he rationalized, "That law was for Jews living in the land, not for us who live among the Gentiles." Elimelech again rationalized, "These girls—Orpah and Ruth— are good, submissive girls, they'll make good wives."

Each year it became harder to leave their new friends in Moab and return to Bethlehem. Without warning one morning, Naomi tried to awaken Elimelech, but he had died in his sleep. The two new families rallied support around Naomi and she endured the shock. *Lord, we don't mean to rebel against Your ways, it's just that we follow our rationalizations rather than seeking Your will in Scripture. Forgive us!*

Seasons piled one upon another for ten years, and then both sons of Naomi died. Orpah and Ruth became widows, just as Naomi. They had friends in Moab to help them, but life was a struggle. Without the two sons to work the land and tend the animals, Naomi quickly lost one possession after another. Then she lost one animal after another.

What would she do? After careful thought, Naomi gathered the two grieving daughters-in-law together to tell them, "I'm going back to Bethlehem; I have family there." Orpah and Ruth cried and agonized. Both young widows in their own way asked, "What can I do, where can I go?" They faced a dreadful crisis. *Lord, prepare me for crisis for it will certainly come.*

Naomi had already thought about her options. She didn't have family in Moab to take care of her. Her friends in Moab treated her like a foreigner, which she was. Rather than starve to death in Moab, she might as well go back to family in Bethlehem and starve there. *Lord, it's amazing how we never consider Your will when making plans for our lives. Forgive our self-inclination.*

Naomi told each daughter-in-law to go back to her mother's house, "Let your family take care of you." Naomi had already decided the fate for each woman.

Early the next morning, Naomi began her trip to Bethlehem. Her two daughters-in-law walked a little distance with her. When they came to a narrow mountain road that led down, it was the obvious place to say good-bye.

Naomi said to each daughter-in-law, "'Go back to your father's house instead of coming with me. May the Lord reward you for your kindness to your husbands and to me. May the Lord bless you with the security of another marriage.'" Then she kissed them good-bye and they all broke down and wept. Orpah kissed her mother-in-law good-bye and turned back. But Ruth insisted on staying with Naomi. *Lord, prepare me to make the correct decisions when hard choices come.*

This is a dismal story of an apparently fine family that tried to care for itself in the recession of hard times. At first it seemed their decision was a wise one, but then one disaster hits after another. Finally desperation sets in, and out of despair comes a young woman—Ruth—who chooses to follow the living God. Since our lives are directed by our choices, Ruth found prosperity and happiness because she chose God. *Lord, may I always make right choices.*

Elimelech and His Family Move to Moab

SCRIPTURE: RUTH 1

During the time of the heroic judges of Israel, there was a famine when crops did not grow and there was nothing to eat in the land. A man from the town of Bethlehem in Judah went to stay in the country of Moab—he, his wife, and his two sons. The man's name was Elimelech. The name of his wife was Naomi, and the names of his two sons were Mahlon and Chilion. They were Ephrathites (an ancient name of the elitist) from Bethlehem in Judah. They went into the country of Moab and stayed there. *Lord, I will not go to places that You condemn.*

Naomi, Orpah, and Ruth Become Widows

Then Elimelech, Naomi's husband, died, and she and her two sons grieved. Later, each of the two sons got married to two women from Moab, one's name was Orpah, and the name of the other one was Ruth. They lived there for about ten years, and then both Mahlon and Chilion died. So Naomi was left without her two sons and her husband. *Lord, I know there are consequences when I live outside Your will.*

Naomi and Ruth Return to Bethlehem

Then Naomi and her daughters-in-law got ready to move, so that Naomi could return home from the country of Moab, because Naomi heard how the Lord helped His people by giving them food. So she and her two daughters-in-law started out from the place where she had been living. They were traveling on the road back to the land of Judah. Then Naomi said to her two daughters-in-law, "Go back. Each of you should return to your mother's house. May the Lord be kind to you, as you have been toward my dead husband and sons, and toward me. May the Lord allow both of you to find new homes, each of you in the house of your new husband." Then Naomi kissed them, and they began to cry loudly. They said to her, "No, we should go with you to Judah, to your people." *Lord, I will never counsel people to go back to their heathen ways.*

But Naomi said, "Turn back, my daughters. Why should you go with me? Do I have any more sons in my womb who could become your husbands? Turn back, my daughters, go your way. I am too old to have another husband. If I were to think: 'I have hope'— even if I should get married tonight and give birth to sons— would you wait until they were old enough? Would you wait to marry them? Of course not, my daughters. It is more bitter for me than for you, because the Lord's hand has gone out against me." *Lord, when I get despondent, I will look beyond my circumstances to You.*

Then the two young women began to cry loudly again. Orpah kissed her mother-in-law good-bye and left, but Ruth continued to cling to Naomi. Naomi said, "Look, your sister-in-law has gone back to her people and to her gods. Follow her." *Lord, Naomi was wrong to send Orpah back to idolatrous gods. May I never counsel this way.*

But Ruth said, "Don't ask me to leave you, or stop following you— because wherever you go, I will go. And wherever you stay, I will stay. Your people will become my people, and your God will be my God. Wherever you die, I will die, and I will be buried there. May the Lord treat me harshly—no matter how harsh it is—if anything except death separates you and me." And when Naomi realized that Ruth was determined to go with her, she said nothing more. So the two of them traveled until they came to the town of Bethlehem. When they arrived there, the whole village was excited because of them. The old women said, "Is this Naomi?" *Lord, I will choose You, as did Ruth.*

Naomi answered them, "Don't call me 'Naomi' (pleasant), because the Almighty God has been harsh to me. Call me 'Mara' (bitter). I went away full, but the Lord has brought me back home empty. Why are you calling me 'Naomi,' since the Lord has afflicted me, and the Almighty God has caused me to suffer?" *Lord, I will recognize the course of my punishment.*

So Naomi returned to Bethlehem, and Ruth, the Moabite woman, her daughter-in-law, was with her. They returned from the country of Moab and came to Bethlehem at the beginning of the time for harvesting barley. *Lord, I marvel at Your providence.*

The Story of Ruth's Choice

Date: 1312 B.C. ❧ Place: Bethlehem

But Ruth said: "Entreat me not to leave you, or to turn back from following after you; for wherever you go, I will go; and wherever you lodge, I will lodge; your people shall be my people, and your God, my God. Where you die, I will die, and there will I be buried. The Lord do so to me, and more also, if anything but death parts you and me" (Ruth 1:16-17).

The road from Moab to Bethlehem is not that long. Twenty miles from somewhere in Moab to the Jordan River which is the boundary between the two nations. Perhaps another 30 miles from there to Bethlehem. But Ruth didn't make a 50 mile trek; her trip was from hell to Heaven, from one end of earth to the center of God's presence. When Ruth decided, "Your God will be my God," it was a decision of complete dedication, and God in Heaven who knows all things took note of Ruth's choice and rewarded her abundantly.

Ruth was poor, with no means of making a living. Ruth was a widow, with no one to love her. Ruth was a foreigner—a Moabite—yet she chose to go to Israel, a place she'd never seen. She chose to go to Bethlehem, a place that previously had a famine. And she chose to go with Naomi, a widow woman also with no hope. But God saw her heart. *Lord, see my heart when I make choices for You.*

Ruth made a decision for God when there was no earthly benefit to being a follower of God. She chose God for the sake of God. "Your God shall be my God." *Lord, I choose You because of who You are.*

Naomi was not a good role model. Naomi bitterly complained, "The Almighty has afflicted me" (Ruth 1:21). Naomi compromised, she wanted Ruth to go back to her heathen gods, "Look, your sister-in-law has gone back to her people and to her gods; return after your sister-in-law" (Ruth 1:15 NKJV). Did you see that, Naomi wanted Ruth to go back to her gods, what kind of spiritual advice is that? *Lord, keep me from listening to spiritual advice from backslidden believers.*

Have you ever been in a hole like Ruth was in? No money! No home! No one to help you! Nothing! Your fear is greater than any other feeling. Your embarrassment is beyond feelings. Poverty is the only assurance you have. When you get there, confess what Ruth confessed, "Your God shall be my God." *Lord, You rejoiced over Ruth's decision, "There is joy by God in the presence of the angels over one sinner that repents"* (Luke 15:10 ELT). *Lord, I rejoice with Your laughter over my conversion.*

Every decision made for God will be tested. The poverty of her mother-in-law was compounded by sorrow. But even in the face of depression, Ruth said, "Your God shall be my God." Naomi told Ruth to count the cost. Naomi said, "I can't have more sons, and if I could, it would be too long before one would be old enough for marriage." Naomi painted a dark picture. Why would Ruth go there? God was the answer. "Your God will be my God." Didn't Jesus remind us to count the cost? "If any one comes after me...they must take up the cross daily" (Luke 9:23 ELT). *Lord, You are worthy of all the persecution.*

When fellow travelers turn back, it's hard to go on. Notice what Ruth and Orpah did together, Naomi's "two daughters-in-law went with her" (Ruth 1:7 NKJV). "We will return with you" (Ruth 1:10 NKJV), and they "wept together" (Ruth 1:14).

The influence of one family member on another is great. Yet in spite of Orpah's turning back and Naomi's negative advice, Ruth said, "Your God shall be my God." *Lord, I will not be separated from You.*

Most people need encouragement to make a good decision. Ruth didn't get encouragement from Naomi or Orpah. She didn't dream of utopia in Bethlehem. She didn't plan on another marriage and children. There wasn't even government subsidy or a welfare program. Nothing. That makes her decision all the greater. "Your God shall be my God." *Lord, I choose You, to live with You, nothing else.*

My Time to Pray

Lord, You use a great church to get people saved; You also use praying friends, or a host of other positive influences that bring them to You.

But Ruth had absolutely no positive incentives To choose You and follow You.

Lord, may I have single vision as Ruth, To choose You rather than anything else.

I will make Naomi's God, my God; I choose to follow You, no matter what.

Amen.

Ruth Works in the Field of Boaz

SCRIPTURE: RUTH 2

Now Naomi had a relative on her husband's side of the family. He was a rich man in the family of Elimelech. His name was Boaz. Ruth, the Moabite woman, said to Naomi, "Allow me to go now to the field and pick up the leftover grain behind whomever gives me the privilege." Naomi said to her, "Go on, my daughter."

So Ruth set out to go and glean (to carefully gather any leftover grain which was missed by the harvesters) in the fields behind the harvesters. She happened to come to the part of the field that belonged to Boaz. He was from the family of Elimelech. Then Boaz came from the town of Bethlehem and said to the harvesters, "May the Lord be with you." And they answered him, "May the Lord bless you." *Lord, I do admire good relations between management and workers.*

Then Boaz asked his servant who supervised the harvesters, "Whose girl is that?" The foreman answered, "She is the Moabite girl who came back with Naomi from the country of Moab. She came and asked me, 'Let me please glean and gather among the stalks of grain behind the harvesters.' She has continued to work hard since early morning until now, except for resting a little while in the workers' hut." *Lord, remind me constantly to work hard at my job.*

Then Boaz said to Ruth, "Listen carefully, my daughter. Do not go to glean in any other field or leave here. Stay close to my workers. Watch the field where the men are harvesting, and follow along behind them. (The men cut the stalks of grain and the women went along behind to gather and bind the stalks into bundles. Ruth was allowed to glean whatever was left.) I have ordered the young men not to bother you. And when you get thirsty, go to our water jars and drink from what the workers have drawn." Then Ruth bowed herself on the ground saying to him, "Why would you be so nice to me? Why would you even notice me? I am a foreigner." *Lord, I will be nice to all.*

Then Boaz answered her, "Everything that you have done for your mother-in-law since the death of your husband has been fully explained to me—how you left your father, your mother, and your native land, to come to a people whom you never knew before now. May the Lord reward your work and may He give you a rich blessing. He is the God of Israel, the one from whom you seek protection under His wings."

Then she said, "You are being nice to me, my master. You have spoken kindly to me and encouraged me, even though I am not one of your own servant girls." *Lord, gratitude is a mark of character.*

At mealtime, Boaz said to her, "Come here, eat some bread and dip your morsel in the wine sauce." Then she sat beside the harvesters. And they passed roasted grain to her. She ate until she was satisfied. She even had some grain left over. And when she got up to glean, Boaz ordered his young men, saying, "Let her glean even among the stalks of grain; and don't embarrass her. Also, be sure to pull out some stalks from the bundles and leave them for her. Allow her to glean, and don't rebuke her." *Lord, I will be kind to the poor as You directed.*

So Ruth gleaned in the fields until evening. Then she threshed what she had gathered and it amounted to about half a bushel of barley. Then she picked it up and brought it into town. Ruth brought it out and gave to Naomi the food that she had left over after being satisfied at mealtime. When Ruth's mother-in-law saw what she had gleaned, she asked her, "Where did you glean today? Where did you work? May the man who took notice of you be blessed."

So Ruth told her mother-in-law, "The man's name whom I worked with today is Boaz." Then Naomi said to her daughter-in-law, "May this man be blessed by the Lord. God has not withdrawn His kindness to those who are alive or dead." Then Naomi said to her, "This man, Boaz, is a relative of ours, one of our closest relatives." (The kinsman-redeemer [Hebrew: go'el] was responsible for protecting members of his extended family who could not help themselves. See Lev. 25:25-28, 47-49.) Ruth, the Moabite woman, said, "Yes, and he even said to me, 'You must stay close to my young men until they have finished harvesting my whole crop.'" *Lord, the way You work between a man and a woman is wonderful.*

Then Naomi said to Ruth, her daughter-in-law, "My daughter, it is good that you will be going out with his workers and that others will not be bothering you in any other field." So Ruth stayed close to the workers of Boaz, gleaning until the end of the barley harvest and the wheat harvest. And Ruth lived with her mother-in-law. *Lord, I marvel at Your care for those who trust You.*

Plans for a Husband

Scripture: Ruth 3

Then Naomi, Ruth's mother-in-law, said to Ruth, "My daughter, shouldn't I look for a home for you, so that it may go well for you? And isn't Boaz our relative? You were with his workmen. Listen, he is winnowing (winnowing is separating the chaff from the grain by throwing it up into the wind) barley tonight at the threshing-floor. So wash, put on some perfume, wear your best clothes, and go down to the threshing-floor. However, do not reveal yourself to the man until he has finished eating and drinking. And when he lies down, you must take note of the place where he lies down. Then you must go in, uncover his feet, and lay down, too. (There was nothing immoral about Ruth's actions. Naomi was advising Ruth to formally ask Boaz to take on the obligation of a close relative. This included marrying Ruth.) He will tell you what to do." *Lord, love always finds a way.*

And Ruth said to her, "I will do everything you say." So, she went down to the threshing-floor as her mother-in-law had told her. And when Boaz had finished eating and drinking, and he was in a good mood, he went to lie down at the far end of the pile of grain. Then Ruth came softly and uncovered his feet, and she lay down. At midnight, the man was startled and turned over. He saw a woman lying at his feet. And Boaz asked, "Who are you?"

She answered, "I am Ruth, your servant girl. Spread your cloak of protection over me (here Ruth is asking Boaz to marry her) because you are a close relative."

Then Boaz said, "May the Lord bless you, my daughter. You have shown more kindness at the end than at the beginning. You did not go after young men, whether rich or poor. And now, my daughter, don't be afraid. I will do for you whatever you ask. All of my fellow townspeople know that you are a noble woman. Now it is true that I am a close relative. However, there is a relative who is closer than I am. Stay here tonight. In the morning, if he will perform the duty of a relative for you, fine. Let him do that. However, if he is unwilling to do this for you, then I will do it—as surely as the Lord lives. Lie down here until morning!" *Lord, You recognize marriage customs in all kinds of cultures.*

So Ruth lay down at his feet until morning. Then she got up early, before anybody could recognize each other. Boaz had said, "Do not let it be known that a woman came to the threshing-floor." He also said, "Bring the shawl that you have on and hold it out." So she held it out. Boaz measured out six units of barley and placed it upon her. Then she went into town. Now when Ruth came to her mother-in-law, Naomi asked, "How did it go, my daughter?" Ruth told her everything that the man had done for her. "Boaz gave me these six units of barley! He said, 'Do not go away empty-handed to your mother-in-law.'"

Then Naomi said, "Wait, my daughter, until you learn how this thing develops. Boaz will not rest until he has settled this matter today." *Lord, You put love in the hearts of men and women for each other. Teach me to love more deeply as You love.*

Boaz Marries Ruth

SCRIPTURE: RUTH 4

Boaz went up to the gate (most of the business transactions were conducted at the town gate, because witnesses were always present) of the town and sat down. The close relative of whom Boaz had spoken came by, Boaz said to him, "Turn aside, my friend; sit down here." So the man sat down. Boaz selected ten men (local Jews who acted as official witnesses to this land transaction) from the elders of the town and said, "Sit down with us." So they sat down. Then Boaz said to the closest relative, "Naomi has returned from the country of Moab and is selling the section of land which belongs to our brother, Elimelech. So I thought I would tell you about this land in the presence of those who sit here and in the presence of the elders of my people. If you want to redeem it, then do so. However, if you choose not to redeem it, then tell me, so that I may know...because there is no one else to redeem it except you. And I am next of kin after you." *Lord, I thank You that Jesus redeemed me from the slavery of sin.*

The man said, "I will redeem it."

Then Boaz said, "On the day that you buy this field from the hand of Naomi, you must also buy it from Ruth, the Moabite woman, who is the widow of Naomi's dead son, in order to restore the name of the dead man to his inheritance." (According to Levirate law, Ruth's firstborn son would keep Mahlon's name alive. The child would later also own the family inheritance.)

Then the close relative said, "I cannot redeem it for myself, because I would endanger my own estate. You take my right of redemption;

I cannot redeem it." *Lord, thank You that Jesus didn't turn back from redeeming me.*

Now it was the custom in earlier times in Israel, in the redemption and exchange of land, to confirm all things of a transaction: A man would take off his shoe and give it to his neighbor. This was the legal proof in Israel. So when that close relative said to Boaz, "Buy it for yourself," the man took off his own shoe. *Lord, the price of my redemption was the blood of Your Son, Jesus Christ.*

Then Boaz announced to the elders and to all of the people: "You are witnesses today that I have purchased from the hand of Naomi everything which belonged to Elimelech and everything which had belonged to Chilion and Mahlon. Also, I have acquired Ruth, the Moabite woman, the widow of Mahlon, to be my wife, in order to raise up the name of her dead husband upon his inheritance, so that the name of the dead man will not disappear from among his brothers or from the gate of his birthplace. You are all witnesses today." Then all of the elders who were at the town gate said, "We are witnesses. May the Lord make Ruth, who is coming into your household, to be like Rachel and Leah. Those two women built up the house of Israel. And may you be a success in Ephratah and become famous in the town of Bethlehem. And may your house be like the house of Perez, whom Tamar gave birth for Judah, through the descendants whom the Lord will give you out of this young woman." *Lord, thank You for Your blessing.*

The Family Record of Boaz

So Boaz took Ruth and she became his wife. He had sexual relations with her, and the Lord enabled her to become pregnant and give birth to a son. Then the neighbor women said to Naomi, "Praise the Lord, He has not left you without a close relative. May the baby's name become famous in Israel. May he be a restorer of life you to. May he be a nourisher in your old age, because your daughter-in-law, Ruth, who loves you, has given birth to him. She is better to you than seven sons. Then Naomi took the child, and laid him in her lap, and became his babysitter. *Lord, thank You for working together the details of this family for Your glory.*

The neighbor women gave him a name, saying, "There is a grandson born to Naomi." And they named him "Obed," who became the father of Jesse, who was later the father of David (the ancestor of Jesus Christ). *Lord, over 1,000 years before Jesus was born, You worked details into Your predetermined plan of the ages.*

Now these are the generations of Perez: Perez fathered Hezron, and Hezron fathered Ram, and Ram fathered Amminadab, and Amminadab fathered Nahshon, and Nahshon fathered Salmon, and Salmon fathered Boaz, and Boaz fathered Obed, and Obed fathered Jesse, and Jesse fathered David.

Lord, may my children follow You as did the children of Boaz and Ruth.

Amen.

Ruth 4

The Story of the Kinsman-Redeemer

Date: 1312 B.C. ✦ Place: Bethlehem

God had a special land called the Promised Land because He promised to give it to Abraham and his seed. Did you see that God promised the land to everyone in the lineage of Abraham? Therefore, every Israelite had a stake in the land, no matter how small the family.

When Joshua conquered the land from heathen nations, he divided it to every family under God's divine guidance. Therefore every Jew's inheritance was inextricably tied to the land.

But sometimes because of recession, famine, or poverty, a few Jews had to sell themselves and/or their land into slavery (see Lev. 25:39-43). Then a near kin (Go'el) was one who had the right or privilege to buy back the property. Hence, he is a redeemer so that the land and inheritance were kept in the family. *Lord, I am a slave sold into sin.*

Boaz is an outstanding example of one who was a near relative of Naomi (Ruth's mother-in-law) who acted within Jewish law to redeem the land and marry Ruth. This is a type that foreshadows Jesus Christ.

God created the world, but Adam and Eve—the head of the human race—sold their inheritance into sin. "As by one man sin entered into the world...and so death passed upon all" (Rom. 5:12). In picture, all after Adam and Eve become slaves to sin and death. *Lord, I need a redeemer.*

Jesus is the Kinsman-Redeemer of the human race. He became flesh to identify with humankind, and then paid the price of sin—His death—so His blood was spilt to redeem all. Jesus paid the price to redeem (buy back) the human race. *Lord, I accept Your redemption and forgiveness.*

My Time to Pray

Lord, You gave me life and freedom and knowledge
To choose to love and follow You.

But I chose to follow the path of self and sin;
I rebelled against You and chose my own way.

Lord, You sent Jesus to be my Kinsman-Redeemer;
He came to be my brother relation (see Heb. 2:11).

Then He took my sin and died for me (see 2 Cor. 5:21);
Jesus paid my sin debt.

Boaz Marries Ruth

Lord, I praise You for Jesus Christ who saved me;
Now I will live and serve Him.

Amen.

ABOUT THE AUTHOR

D R. ELMER TOWNS is an author of popular and schol-
arly works, a seminar lecturer, and dedicated worker
in Sunday school. He has written over 125 books, including several best sellers. He won the coveted Gold
Medallion Book Award for *The Names of the Holy Spirit.*
Dr. Elmer Towns also cofounded Liberty University with
Jerry Falwell in 1971 and now serves as Dean of the B.R. Lakin School
of Religion and as professor of Theology and New Testament.

Liberty University is the fastest growing Christian university in America.
Located in Lynchburg, Virginia, Liberty University is a private, coeduca-
tional, undergraduate and graduate institution offering 38 undergraduate
and 15 graduate programs serving over 39,000 resident and external stu-
dents (11,300 on campus). Individuals from all 50 states and more than
70 nations comprise the diverse student body. While the faculty and stu-
dents vary greatly, the common denominator and driving force of Liberty
University since its conception is love for Jesus Christ and the desire to
make Him known to the entire world.

For more information about Liberty University, contact:

**Liberty University
1971 University Boulevard
Lynchburg, VA 24502
Telephone: 434-582-2000
Website: www.Liberty.edu**

Dr. Towns's e-mail: www.eltowns@liberty.edu.

Additional copies of this book and other
book titles from DESTINY IMAGE are
available at your local bookstore.

Call toll-free: 1-800-722-6774.

Send a request for a catalog to:

Destiny Image® Publishers, Inc.

P.O. Box 310
Shippensburg, PA 17257-0310

*"Speaking to the Purposes of God for This
Generation and for the Generations to Come."*

For a complete list of our titles,
visit us at www.destinyimage.com.